D1432310

Anglo-Norman
Language & Literature

by

JOHAN VISING

PROFESSOR OF ROMANCE LANGUAGES IN THE UNIVERSITY OF GÖTEBORG

GREENWOOD PRESS, PUBLISHERS
WESTPORT, CONNECTICUT

Originally published in 1923
by Oxford University Press, London

First Greenwood Reprinting 1970

Library of Congress Catalogue Card Number 74-110879

SBN 8371-4560-0

Printed in the United States of America

PREFATORY NOTE

THE Anglo-Norman language and Anglo-Norman literature have hitherto been treated either as a part of the
English language and literature or as an appendix to
French grammar and literary history. An attempt is here
made to present Anglo-Norman as an independent subject.

It is a first attempt and should be judged as such. The
preparatory investigations necessary for a complete compre-
hension of this vast subject are not yet concluded. Though
much has been published in editions of texts, articles, and
monographs—among which those of Paul Meyer must be
given the first place—there are facts, especially facts of
literary import, that have yet to come to light. In this
manual the author has endeavoured to bring together in a
few pages the principal results of the researches that have
been made, gathering up the fruits of his own studies,
which have extended over many years.

The author is greatly indebted to the general editor of
the Oxford Language and Literature Series, Mr. C. T.
Onions, who has collaborated with him throughout. Professor Paul Studer, Dr. Oelsner, Miss Mildred K. Pope,
and many others also have a claim upon his profound
gratitude by the important services they have so kindly
rendered him.

J. V.

CONTENTS

Part I. The Anglo-Norman Language

Part II. Anglo-Norman Literature

Contents

I. THE EXTERNAL HISTORY OF ANGLO NORMAN

§ 1. French immigration in the two hundred years following the Conquest.

BEFORE the Norman Conquest French manners and the French language had exercised a considerable influence on the higher grades of society in England, and a great number of French officials, merchants, and craftsmen had already settled there. 'When William visited England in 1051, he might almost have imagined himself in his own country: Normans commanded the ships, Norman soldiers composed the garrison of Canterbury; other Normans, officers and priests, did him homage' (Glasson, *Histoire du droit et des institutions politiques ... de l'Angleterre*, i. 372). The state of England in 1066 was therefore comparable to the state of Gaul before Caesar's conquest. 'Referta Gallia negotiatorum est, plena ciuium Romanorum', says Cicero (*Pro Fonteio*, v). This early influx of Normans into the country in no small measure prepared the ground for William's conquest.

The magnitude of William's invading army made a great impression upon the English, and its numbers, as well as the numbers of the Norman feudal lords installed during his reign, were greatly exaggerated. Geffrey Gaimar (*Estorie*, l. 5248), probably following tradition, gives the number of the Conqueror's ships as 11,000 (one manuscript has 9,000), while Wace (*Roman de Rou*, l. 6453) states that he has read that they numbered 3,000, but that his father told him there were 696 (l. 6447). Ordericus Vitalis estimates the number of the feudal lords at the excessive figure of 60,000 (Stubbs, *Constitutional History*, i. 287). The size of William's army has been very variously estimated (see Freeman, *Norman Conquest,* iii. 389); the number 50,000 given by William of Poitiers and other authorities is certainly too high; on the other hand, the six to seven thousand suggested by Spatz (*Hist. Studien*, 1896) must be an under-estimate. A more reasonable estimate is the 12,000 assigned by Geoffry Hill (*Consequences of the Norman Conquest*, 19), or the 10,000 to 15,000 suggested by Baring and adopted by Hodgkin in *The Political Hist. of England*, i. 486. If William provided five thousand of his knights with fiefs (J. H. Round, *The Commune of London and other Studies*, p. 289), and the number of the fallen amounted to some thousands, Hill's estimate seems to be justified.

Immediately after his victory William drafted to England a great number of Cluniac and Augustinian monks, whom he appointed to ecclesiastical and scholastic offices. Frenchmen of all classes came over in thousands and occupied important posts, whether in the court, in noble households, or as teachers and skilled workmen in the service of the Church. 'The Norman townsman and the Norman merchant followed hard upon the Norman armies, in the Norman colony in London, in the traders of the ports, in the boroughs of the western border' (Haskins, *The Normans in European History*, p. 81). In this way about 200,000 Frenchmen settled in England during the Conqueror's reign (Hill, op. cit., p. 24).

To this invasion of the French there corresponded a systematic suppression and diminution of the English element.

> Li reis amat mult ses Normanz;
> Les Engleis enueia as chans,
> As perilz e a la folie;
> Guaires ne li fud de lur uie.

So says Adgar in his twenty-second *Legend* (ed. Neuhaus, p. 136). A considerable part of the English population perished in the war, in insurrections, by execution, or by flight. It has been calculated that of the English population, reckoned at the most at two millions, the fourth part were killed or otherwise disappeared during William I's reign (Hill, op. cit., p. 24). 'England became a part of France and thus entered fully into the life of the world to which France belonged' (Haskins, op. cit., p. 82).

This immigration from France and the consequent subjugation of the English continued with greater or less intensity for some two hundred years. The ruling classes were constantly recruited from France, especially from Normandy. The accession of the Angevins and the troubles of Stephen's reign were highly favourable to this incessant

French invasion.   At this king's death not less than 1,115 strongholds were in the hands of Norman barons. When John Lackland had lost his French provinces, a great many Frenchmen, who would not accommodate themselves to the new conditions in France, came over to England, and John encouraged them with all his power.   A chronicler states that he went so far in this ' ut totam Anglorum progeniem funditus ab Anglia eradicaret et barbaris nationibus terram perpetuam possidendam donaret '.

William the Marshal, Earl of Pembroke, Henry III's regent, had a more national policy; but Henry's own rule was as antinational as it could be.   The Poitevin Peter des Roches, bishop of Winchester, came into power in 1232; he called in two thousand Poitevins and Bretons and provided them with remunerative offices or with rich marriages. When two years later Peter fell from power, Henry, though born and educated in England and boasting of his English birth, confided himself to other foreigners, whose transference to this country was furthered still more by the king's marriage in 1236 with Eleanor of Provence. The king now lavished his favour on the queen's Provençal and Savoy compatriots, and especially on her eight uncles. ' England was now the hunting-ground of any well-born Frenchmen anxious for a wider career than they could obtain at home' (Tout in *The Political History of England*, iii. 55).   When Henry's mother Isabelle, who as a widow had married the count of Lusignan, died in 1246, her younger sons, the king's half-brothers, and ' any Poitevin, even if not a member of the house of Lusignan ', were welcomed to England.   ' The alien invasion took a newer and more grievous shape.'

The influx of foreign mercenaries was constant, though their stay in the country was frequently a short one.   From the Conquest onwards, kings as well as barons had recruited their armies with soldiers from abroad both in their insular and their continental wars.   Thus did William Rufus in order to repel an invasion of Canute; Stephen in his long wars against Maud, and Maud herself, and the barons who were loyal to her, in the same war; Henry, son of Henry II, in his war against his father; King John during the whole of his reign, and even Henry III in the years 1232 and 1233. Such bands of mercenaries, however, made no long stay and were several times expelled from England, as for instance at the beginning of Henry II's reign and under the regency of William of Pembroke. Many of these mercenaries came from the north of France and therefore were generally called Brabançons (see Fantosme's *Chron.*, ed. Michel, pp. 4, 10).

A longer, or rather a permanent, stay was made by most of the monks and clergymen who were brought over from France to take possession of ecclesiastical offices, to found monasteries, or to perform the functions of preaching and teaching to which the religious orders devoted themselves.

As has been said, a considerable number of Cluniac and Augustinian monks were invited to England by the Conqueror. In later times the number of these monks increased greatly. They came more especially from Normandy, which by the end of Henry I's reign had sent to England seventeen colonies of Cluniac monks; and there were in England at this time about fifty Augustinian monasteries. Next came the Cistercians, who had fifty monasteries in England, chiefly in the northern counties. In the thirteenth century England received large numbers of Franciscans and Dominicans, and about the middle of the thirteenth century these two orders possessed forty-nine establishments with 1,242 members (Thomas de Eccleston, *De adventu fratrum*, cap. ii).

These monks and friars exercised a very great influence because they spread over the whole of the country and mingled with the common people as preachers and teachers or as farmers and labourers. It is true that some Englishmen entered these orders, but they were few, and it is doubtful whether they used any other language than that of their French brethren. There are indeed, in the thirteenth century, regulations prescribing that Latin or French should be the colloquial language of religious communities.

While these religious provided elementary instruction, other foreigners were employed as professors and lecturers at the universities, and there was an interchange of students between Paris and Oxford. Many such teachers

came at the invitation of King Stephen, and in the reign
of Henry III French scholars came over in large numbers,
'ad mille usque (vel ut aliqui volunt ad diversa millia)',
according to Wood's *Hist. Universitatis Oxon.* (i. 83).

Other classes of immigrants are less remarkable.   There
were continual accessions of tradesmen and artisans, especially Walloons, and among them a considerable number
of Jews, who found in London a suitable field for their
activities.

§ 2. The diffusion of the French language in England.

As at the time of the Conqueror and his immediate
successors the ruling and cultivated classes were almost
exclusively recruited by people of French descent and
a great part of the working population was of the same
extraction, the French language naturally acquired a position of dominance and became widely diffused in England.
To the same effect tended the whole policy of the first
Norman kings.   The Conqueror's court consisted exclusively of French people.   He provided his French soldiers
with fees in all parts of England.   He appointed Frenchmen to all the higher offices in State and Church, and when
he appointed his friend Lanfranc to the primacy of the
English Church he directed a fatal blow against the English
clergy.   This favouring of the French continued for almost
two hundred years, and French remained the language of
the Court even into the fifteenth century.

In the courts of justice French soon became the obliga-
tory language.   It is true that the old English law remained
in force, but this fact could not hinder the introduction of
French forms (Pollock and Maitland, *Hist. Engl. Law*,
i. 80 ff.).   The judges belonged, almost without exception, to
French families; the legal terminology was mostly French
or Latin, as was also the judicial literature.   It follows that
the pleadings would be conducted in Anglo-Norman.[1]
This is confirmed by the difficulty experienced at a later
period of introducing English as the language of the Law

[1] An example of these pleadings is given by Maitland, *Year Books
of Edw. II*, i, Introd., p. xv.

Courts, of which we shall have to speak later. Robert Holcot, who wrote early in the fourteenth century, says of the Conqueror that he 'ordinavit quod nullus in curia regis placitaret nisi in Gallico'. Some modern scholars, such as Gneist, Maitland, and Behrens, have called his trustworthiness in question ; but he bases his statement on older authorities, and there seem to be no real grounds for doubting his reliability. It is probable that there were advocates or interpreters speaking both English and French (cf. Horwood, *Year Books of* [30 and 31] *Edward I*, 1863, p. xxv ; see also Freeman, *Hist. Norman Conq.* v. 407, 413, 423 ; Stubbs, *Const. Hist.*, 1897, i. 290 seq.).

The old English laws were translated into Latin in the first instance, and later into French. Similarly, new laws were issued first in Latin, then in French. The first French or Anglo-Norman laws are those called *Leges* (or *Leis e custumes*) *Willelmi Conquestoris* (ed. Matzke, 1899). The original of these laws seems to date from about the beginning of the twelfth century ; Matzke places it in the period 1150–1170 (Introd., p. lii), but other critics assign an earlier date (cf. Bémont's Préface and *Romania*, xxix. 154 ; *Literaturblatt für germ. und rom. Philologie*, 1901, 119). It is not, however, until the second half of the thirteenth century that laws are ordinarily drawn up in Anglo-Norman. Such laws are to be found in *Statutes of the Realm*, from 1275. It is a matter of course that debates in Parliament were held in French (Pollock and Maitland, op. cit., i. 83), though petitions were for a long time drawn up in Latin. The first Anglo-Norman parliamentary writ is of the date 1274–5 and the first petition of the date 1278 (*Rolls of Parliament*).

The instruction in schools was given in French, as is stated by Holcot, himself a teacher. He complains that children first learn French, and after French the Latin language. This he observes to have been a practice introduced by the Conqueror and to have remained ever since (Warton, *Hist. Engl. Poetry*, p. 11). The same facts are stated by Higden (*Polychronicon*, Rolls ed. ii. 159).

The great majority of the clergy must have preached in French or in Latin, as they were bound to use these languages in conversation. The Constitutions of Clarendon (1164) forbade sons of a villain, that is, in general, native Englishmen, to become priests. The necessary consequence of this prohibition was that there were very few priests capable of preaching in English. That the hearers did not understand the French (or the Latin) of the preacher was no bar to his using these languages, for it is related of Giraldus Cambrensis that, when he once preached in Wales in French and Latin, his auditors did not understand him, but came, notwithstanding, in crowds (*De Rebus a se gestis*, cap. xviii) to respond to his call to engage in the crusades. Yet, there were at all periods some preachers who addressed their hearers in English. The English literature of the twelfth century is chiefly homiletical. In Jocelin de Brakelond's chronicle, anno 1200, there is a statement that the sermons were delivered ' Gallice vel pocius Anglice, ut morum fieret edificacio, non literature ostensio' (ed. Camden Society, 1840, p. 95).

Official and private letters, covenants, charters, and other deeds continued for a long time to be written in Latin. Anglo-Norman epistolary literature does not begin before the middle of the thirteenth century. Later in that century it becomes very abundant, and still more in the first half of the fourteenth century (see Tanquerey, *Recueil de lettres*, p. xi). A short letter written in French by Stephen Langton, in 1215, is unique for the time ; another official letter, written by Peter de Montfort in 1256, is published in Rymer's *Foedera*.

In the sequel, the French language took possession of the literature in England—religious as well as secular—and became the common language of all practical intercourse. The history of Anglo-Norman literature will be set out in Part II, where it will be shown how rich it was in the twelfth and thirteenth centuries, whereas English literature is scanty and of poor quality during the first century after the Conquest. Here follows a series of quotations to illustrate the extent and popularity of the Anglo-Norman language even among the unlearned.[1]

[1] Most of these passages have been cited in my article in *Minnesskrift*, &c. (1920).

The earliest testimony is that of Hue de Rotelande in his *Ipomedon*, about 1175 (ll. 25-32):

> Ne di pas q'il bien ne dit
> Cil qi en latin l'ad descrit,
> Mes plus i ad *leis* ke lettrez;
> Si li latin n'est translatez,
> Gaires n'i erent entendanz;
> Por ceo voil jeo dire en romanz
> A plus brevement qe jeo saurai
> Si entendrunt et clerc et *lai*.

In other places, approximately contemporaneous, we find similar statements. Thus, in Denis Piramus's *Vie Seint Edmund* (ll. 3267-70):

> Translaté l'ai desqu'a la fin
> E de l'engleis e del latin
> Q'en franceis le poent entendre
> Li grant, [li mien] e *li mendre*.

Here, it is to be observed, the translation is made from English in order to be understood by *li mendre*, the lower orders.

In Guischart de Beauliu's translation into French of a sermon, the translator says (ll. 7, 8):

> Jeo larrei le latin sil dirrai en romanz:
> Cil *ki ne sunt gramaires* ne seient pas dutanz

(they who are unlearned need not be afraid).

A long explanation is given by the author of a *Vie de Saint Clément*, about 1200, where we read (*Not. et Extr. des Manuscrits*, xxxviii. 314):

> Li clerc meisme ki funt ces livres
> Prest ne sunt ne delivres
> De faire as *nun lettrez aprendre*
> E en *vulgar cumun entendre*
> Que ceo seit que il unt dit . . .
> Al mien avis mult mieuz serreit
> E a plus grant pru turnereit
> Si li livre de antiquité . . .
> En tel language tresturné fussent
> Que plusurs gent pru en eussent
> Ne sui pas de ces lettrez
> Ki en clergie sunt fundez

Nepurquant cel poi que sai
De si escrivre en purpos ai
Que clerc e *lai* qui l'orrunt
Bien entendre le porrunt,
Si si vilains del tut ne seient
Que puint de rumanz apris n'aient.

In the last two lines the author gives us to understand that there were *vilains*, very illiterate people, that did not know French.

In a letter of 1209 to Giraldus Cambrensis Walter Map complains that he has not used the *common language*, that is the French, which would have secured a greater popularity for his works (*Opera Giraldi*, v. 410). In a legendary of about the same date (MS. Roy. 20, B. xiv, Brit. Mus.) the author says (fol. 108, vº. 2) that he addresses himself to ' clerk e *lai*, veil et enfant ' (see Kjellman, *Studier i modern Språkvetenskap*, v. 218). The following quotations are also from the first half of the thirteenth century :

Ço est de Vitas Patrum, issi cum je l'entent,
Que translaté fu par devin espirement
Al Temple de la Bruere tut veraiment,
Nient pur les clers mes pur *la laie gent,*
Que par le rumanz le *entendent uniement,*[1]
Tut ces que entendre nel sevent autrement.
                    Henry d'Arcy (*Not. et Extr.* XXXV. i. 140).

De latin la dei estrere
E pur *lais* en romans fere.
Le Purgatoire de Saint Patrice (ll. 9, 10, ed. Vising in *Göteborgs Högskolas Årsskrift*, 1916).

Mais clerc e *lai communeaument*
Solent user romanz sovent ;
Pur ço voil en romanz parlier.
La Vie de Saint Eustache (*Not. et Extr.* XXXIV. i. 227).

Si com en latyn le trouai, bon est que ieo le vous die
En fr)unceis pur lez vnes qi ne seiiunt de clergie.
                    La Vision de Tondale (ll. 3, 4).

Pur ceus et celes ki n'entendent quant oient lire le latin
Jeo ai comencé icest livre, e Deus i mette bone fin.
                    La Plainte de Notre Dame (*Rom.* xv. 309).

[1] By *uniement* the author means ' universally.'

Hors de latym le fist atrere
Pur ceux que ne sevent guere
De la force de clergye ;
Pur ceo le fyst, ne dutez mye,
Pur *les layes* muth encenser
C'il (= S'il) le voillent escoter.
Le Mariage des neuf filles du diable (*Rom.* xxix. 61).

En romanz comenz ma reson
Pur ceus ki ne sevent mie
Ne lettreüre ne clergie.
(*Chasteau d'Amour*, 26 seq.)

A royal charter of 1233 (see Thommerel, *Recherches sur la fusion du franco-normand et de l'anglo-saxon*, p. 20) states that the English law terms have been translated into French in order to make them intelligible to everybody.

Again, about the year 1250, Robert of Gretham, an Englishman, addresses himself to *laïs* in French, as the language that is best understood by them. Even an English priest, who is but little versed in French, translates a Latin poem into *romanz*, because he is desirous of serving *la laie gent* (*Sur l'Antechrist* in *Rom.* xxix. 80). Rauf de Lenham says, in 1256, that he has written his *Calendar*, not for clergymen, but for *laie gent* (Paul Meyer, *Doc. manuscrits*, 130).

Pierre de Peckham (or d'Abernun) wrote his French *Lumière as laïs* in 1267-8 (see *Rom.* viii. 325, xv. 288 ; *Rev. langues rom.* liii. 246), and dedicates it, at the end, to *vieux et joevenes, femmes e enfanz*. A little later the same author composed his *Vie de Seint Richard*, wherein he says :

mes de plusurs est desiré
que fust en franceis translaté
ke *laïs* (= aux laïques) entendable pot estre

(ll. 51 ff. in Baker's edition, *Revue des langues romanes*, liii. 316). These testimonies of Pierre's are the more remarkable as he was evidently an Englishman by birth and was not fully master of the French language (cf. ' en franceis au meuz ke jeo say ', *Seint Richard*, l. 62).

B

In a poem on piety, of the second half of the thirteenth century, the author says: 'Si est le Evangel translaté hors de latin en franceys a l'aprise de *lay gent*' (Michel, *Rapports*, 1838, p. 256). At the close of the thirteenth century Wilham de Wadington declares that he has written his *Manuel des pechez* for *la laie gent* (l. 113, ed. Furnivall), and the great number of manuscripts (at least fifteen) preserved testifies to the popularity and wide dissemination of this work.

Finally Nicholas Bozon, about 1300, declares in his *Proverbs* (ed. Furnivall, *Minor Poems of the Vernon MS.*, E.E.T.S. 117, p. 522):

> Ke en escripture ai trové
> E de latin translaté
> En *comun langage* pur amis
> Ke de clergie ne ount apris.

It cannot be denied that these statements furnish a very strong proof of the complete dominance of the Anglo-Norman language during the second half of the twelfth and most of the thirteenth century in nearly all conditions of life, and of its penetration even into the lower strata of society.

§ 3. The Decline of Anglo-Norman.

We have seen in the previous sections how men of French descent took possession of all important positions, how they invaded commerce and the crafts, and how French (Anglo-Norman) spread among all classes. The conditions of things were profoundly changed in consequence of the national movement in the reign of Henry III. This movement was, originally and primarily, concentrated in hostility to the foreigners and the favour shown them by the king, as by his predecessors. The Provisions of Oxford (1258) formulate in official language the hatred of the foreigner that was borne in every good Englishman's breast, and that often finds expression in the literature of the time. The letters of Grosseteste, for example, are full of this hatred (see especially Letter cxxxi, an. 1252, in which he attacks the foreign clergy). The *Annales monastici* have, under the year 1258, the following item: 'Many a one who knew the secret thoughts of the foreigners, believed that, if their power should be greater, they would poison all noblemen in the country, depose the king, and thus bring into subjection the whole country. Moreover, four of the king's brothers, rising vastly above other foreigners in riches and dignity, treat the English with intolerable insolence and do them all sorts of mischiefs,' &c. Similar opinions are pronounced by others, such as Matthew Paris in his *Chronica majora*, v. 363, and the author of the poem *Richard Coer de lyon* (end of the thirteenth century).

The Provisions insisted upon a clean sweep of the aliens, but Henry was at first disposed to withdraw from his engagements. He was, however, soon obliged to confirm them, first in the year 1263, then in the following year after his defeat at Lewes. Shortly after his victory at the battle of Evesham (1265) he recalled some of his favourites, but the original agreement between the king and his subjects was once more corroborated by the Provisions of Marlborough (1267).

Thus a stop was put to the invasions *en masse* of Frenchmen. If, after this, French scholars or students came over to England, they did not on the whole delay the decline of the French language. At most they made individual contributions to French literature in England or taught their language to a few pupils.

An important fact in the rebellion against Henry III was that the rebels consisted not only of the magnates with the Frenchman Simon de Montfort at their head, but also of the lower people, particularly the townsfolk, representing for the most part the English element. This marks a consolidation of the English nation, which was beginning to be conscious of its unity in the face of foreign countries. A proof thereof is that to the Parliament of 1265 not only the magnates were summoned, but also representatives of the counties, towns, and boroughs. An entirely national Parliament, the famous model Parliament, was summoned by Edward I (1295), who has been called the first national king of England.

It is true that a wave of nationalism had swept over England after the loss of Normandy in 1204 (cf. Freeman,

v. 703; Stubbs, i. 558), but to maintain, as is done by some scholars, that the loss of Normandy caused or accelerated the decay of the Anglo-Norman language, is not in accordance with historical facts. There came, as a consequence of this loss, new swarms of French to England, with the necessary result of a reinforcement of the dominant French element, and Anglo-Norman literature becomes much richer in the thirteenth century than before, while the native English literature continues to be comparatively meagre.

It was the rebellion against Henry III, originally directed, as has been said, against his favouritism of foreigners, that brought about the change in the relations between Anglo-Norman and English. English had not perished, though by this time it had fallen very low. Of its status at that time the same may be said as Ranulphus Higden said of it in the fourteenth century : ' in paucis adhuc agrestibus vix remansit' (*Polychronicon,* ii. 160). We have already seen a proof of its tenacity in the sermons of the twelfth century and in a passage of Jocelin de Brakelond (above, p. 14). But the best proof of the vitality of the vernacular idiom is its own character, as exhibited when it had regained its ancient position. It had been very much influenced in the vocabulary, and development has taken place in the pronunciation and in the forms, but it had maintained its grammatical structure, its syntax, the old pronouns, numerals, prepositions, and, on the whole, its basic elements.

In the second half, or rather the last third, of the thirteenth century, are to be found various passages in English literature relating to the status of French and English in the different strata of society.

The prologue of *Richard Coer de lyon* (cf. above, p. 19), which is very hostile, it is true, to the French, has the following passage (ll. 21–4) :

> In Frensshe bookys this rym is wrought,
> Lewede menne knowe it nought,
> Lewede menne cunne French non,
> Among an hondryd unnethis on.

The author of *Arthour and Merlin,* in a passage of twelve lines (18–29) dealing with the languages current in

England, says: 'Those who know French and Latin have advantages. .... It is right that those who were born in England should understand English; I have seen many a noble man who could not speak a French word: for their sake will I tell my tale ... in English.'

Robert of Gloucester has a passage in his *Metrical Chronicle* to the following effect (ed. W. A. Wright, ll. 7538 seq.): 'The Normans only spoke their own language, French, as they did at home, and taught it to their children, so that great men ('heiemen') in this country who descend from their blood retain the speech which they received from them. For if a man does not know French he is little esteemed, but low-born people hold still to English and their own language.'

We read in the *Cursor Mundi* (ll. 232 ff.): 'This book is translated into English for the sake of the English people in England and to be understood by the common people. Here I read French poems commonly everywhere. They are made chiefly for Frenchmen, but what use are they to those who do not know French? The English people of England are in general English; one ought to speak the language in which one best makes one's self understood ... I write for the unlearned English people who understand what I relate.'

The copyist of a manuscript of Luce de Gast says that he knows French badly, as he was born in England (Ward, *Catalogue of Romances*, i. 358).

It is almost superfluous to cite similar passages from the fourteenth century. The following will suffice.

William of Nassyngton in his *Speculum Vite* has a lengthy passage explaining the reasons for his writing in English; among others are the following lines (see *Englische Studien*, vii. 469):

In English tonge I schal ȝow telle

.   .   .   .   .

No Latyn wil I speke no waste,
But English, þat men vse mast,
Þat can eche man vnderstande,
Þat is born in Ingelande;
For þat langage is most chewyd,

Os wel among lered os lewyd.

.   .   .   .   .

And somme can Frensche and no Latyn,
Þat vsed han cowrt and dwellen þerein.

.   .   .   .   .

Boþe lered and lewed, old and ȝonge,
Alle vnderstonden english tonge.

Robert Mannyng, in his version of Wace's Chronicle, finished in 1338, declares that he put forth his history ' not for þe lerid bot for þe lewed ' (Rolls ed., 1. 6).

Some of the passages quoted above show that from the latter part of the thirteenth century even the learned and the ruling classes, or, as the *Cursor Mundi* has it, all, understood English.   It must, indeed, have been the fact that by about 1250 English was well on the way towards the recovery of its position as the common language of ordinary intercourse.   In part proof of this we have the revival and development of English literature during the second half of the thirteenth century (see, for instance, Schofield, *English Literature from the Norman Conquest to Chaucer*, *Appendix I*, *Chronological Table*, p. 461) ; during this period religious works in the vernacular become more numerous, and chronicle and romance make their appearance.   In the following century it was found necessary to encourage the use of French (by the side of Latin) among the learned, for Oxford students are enjoined to use these languages in conversation (see Maxwell Lyte, *History of the University of Oxford*) ; and an official document of 1362 says that French has become an unfamiliar tongue (see below, p. 23).

French, of course, held its position at Court for a long time.   If the first three Edwards understood English, which is doubtful (see Pauli, *Bilder aus Alt-England*, p. 177), they made scant use of it.   Henry IV seems to have been the first king after the Conquest of whom it could be said that English was his native language (*Rolls of Parliament*, III, No. 53).   The fashion of the Court was closely followed by the nobility and official classes, of whom it is said that they sent their sons to France to learn French, and for whom a great number of *Manières de langage* and other manuals were composed.

As the aristocracy and the learned occupied the great offices in Church and State, French naturally held its own in official life; legal terms and formulae were mostly in French, so that the alien tongue was necessarily maintained in courts of justice. In 1362 it was ordered, by an Act of Parliament (drawn up in French), that 'in any courts whatsoever' all pleas should be 'pleaded, shown, defended, answered, debated and judged' in English, on the ground that 'la lange Franceis qest trope desconue' caused great 'harms and mischiefs' (*Statutes of the Realm*, i. 375; cf. Pollock and Maitland, *Hist. Engl. Law*, i. 85). But it was found to be almost impossible to carry out this order. More than a hundred years later Fortescue states that the judges were wont to conduct legal proceedings in French (*De laudibus legum Angliae*, cap. 48). According to Giry (*Manuel de diplomatique*, p. 473), Cromwell abolished French in lawsuits, but this 'novelty' was in its turn abrogated by Charles II. 'The Law is scarcely expressible properly in English' (*Cambridge Hist. Engl. Lit.* i. 408).

It was not until 1731 that the records of lawsuits were regularly written down in English (instead of French or Latin); but the bill in which this was proposed met with vigorous opposition. It was pointed out that with a change of the judicial language the old Records would be neglected and serious inconveniences of all sorts would result (Cobbett, *Parliamentary History*, viii. 858). Law Reports and Cases were drawn up in what is known as 'Law French' down to the eighteenth century (cf. below, ch. vi).

Laws and decrees are written either in French or in Latin until 'late in the fourteenth century, when English begins to make an insidious attack . . . The transition from French to English statutes seems to occur suddenly at the accession of Richard III and to be contemporaneous with a change in the method of enrolment', Pollock and Maitland, op. cit., p. 86 (cf. *Proceedings and Ordinances of the Privy Council of England*, ed. Sir Harry Nicolas).

English was used for the first time at the opening of Parliament in 1363; it was used again in 1365, but not in 1377 (Stubbs, *Const. Hist.* ii. 434). Henry IV addressed a short English speech to his first parliament. It is clear that at that time English was used as well as French in debates, though there does not seem to be any mention of it in historical works. Neither is there any statement of the time when French finally disappeared from the debates. Mätzner (*Englische Grammatik*, i. 6) says it was in the second half of the fourteenth century, in the Commons, and in 1483 in the House of Lords, but this is difficult to establish (cf. Behrens, p. 954). The records of parliament were mostly drawn up in French until the middle of the fifteenth century; in the course of the following century English or Latin came to be more and more used. A few French phrases have been retained in parliamentary procedure down to recent times: 'Le roi le veult', 'Le roi s'avisera', &c. (Scheibner, p. 26).

Petitions to Parliament were written in French, seldom in Latin or English, until the middle of the fifteenth century. 'As early as 1386 ... a petition to parliament might be written in English (*Rot. Parl.* iii. 225), and the English words which Henry IV spoke when he met his first parliament are enrolled (iii. 423); then petitions in English appear on the roll; but on the whole it is not until 1425 or thereabouts that the parliament roll has much English on it' (Pollock and Maitland, p. 86, n. 3).

In official and private letters French was constantly in use over a long period (see Tanquerey, *Recueil de lettres*, Introd.). There are in Rymer's *Foedera*, Part V, several royal and other letters in Anglo-Norman down to 1440, when Latin becomes the usual epistolary language. English is still rare. Wills were made chiefly in Latin; the earliest French wills in the Publications of the Surtees Society (Nos. 2, 4, 26) date from 1347; the earliest English wills from 1383 (see Furnivall, *The fifty earliest English Wills*). It is only in the following century that French yields to English, whereas Latin always prevails.

In schools the substitution of English for French or Latin is late. A passage of Higden's *Polychronicon* has been often quoted as evidence of the language employed in tutorial instruction. From the Conquest onwards, he says, the pupils were obliged to learn French and neglect their native tongue, contrary to the custom of other nations.

Gentlemen's children are taught to speak French from their cradle; the countryfolk people try with all might to imitate them. Trevisa, commenting upon Higden, says: 'Such was the fashion until the first plague (1348); since then a change has been brought about by the schoolmaster John Cornwaile, who made his pupils construe in English instead of French. Richard Pencriche and others after him adopted this method, so that now (in 1385) the children in all the grammar schools of England have given up French and are instructed in English. . . . Even the nobility have now ceased to teach their children French' (*Polychronicon*, ed. Rolls, ii. 159 ff.).

It has been said before (p. 22) that the students of Oxford were ordered to use French or Latin in conversation, which proves that they were rather inclined to speak English. The decrees concerning this date from 1322 to 1340.

The history of the French language in Ireland after the annexation is similar. In some respect it may have more strongly resisted the revival of English, which naturally had a weaker hold in Ireland than in England. Thus it seems that French continued longer to be the judicial language in Ireland than in England (Statutes up to 1508; cf. Behrens, op. cit., p. 954).

In Scotland also French was used by the upper classes and in official and private documents. French was carried into Scotland by monks and traders, by Anglo-Norman immigrants from the beginning of the reign of David I (1124), and later in consequence of the intercourse with France and with England from the time of Edward I onwards. Public Acts in French are found in *The Acts of Parliament of Scotland* (1280–1320). French was taught in schools (see John Edgar, *History of early Scottish Education*, 301; cf. pp. 123, 302, &c.), but it was as much continental French as Anglo-Norman that was learnt.

The dialect of Guernsey and Jersey is not Anglo-Norman, but Norman; see Fleury in *Revue des patois*, iii. 286; and Eggert in *Zeitschrift f. rom. Philologie*, xiii. 353 ff.

The decline of Anglo-Norman in private and public use is due, in a certain degree, to the degeneration of the language and its loss of regularity and stability. Foreign and English influences, individual peculiarities, and the ignorance and negligence of many of those who spoke and wrote Anglo-Norman necessarily had a deteriorating effect on it. Some generations before the external decline of Anglo-Norman manifests itself there are admissions by authors which indicate its internal decay, in the loss of regular and natural development. These statements begin to appear in Anglo-Norman texts about the middle of the thirteenth century and continue for a century and a half. They will be quoted here in chronological order.

In the year 1245 :

> Language par païs varie ;
> Si language de France die,
> N'en doi estre a droit repris
> De gent de veisin païs.
> (*Life of Edward the Confessor*, ed. Luard, ll. 93 ff.)

About 1250 :

> Si rien i ad a amender
> U del fraunceis u del rimer,
> Nel tenés pas a mesprisoun
> Mes bien gardez la raisoun.
> (Robert of Gretham, *Miroir des domées*, in *Rom.* xv. 300.)

In the second half of the thirteenth century :

> Jeo ne sai guers romanz faire
> Ne de latyn ma sermon traire,
> Car jeo ne fu unques a Parys
> Ne al abbaye de saint Denys,
> Pur ceo nul homme ne me doit blamer
> Si jeo ne sai mye bien roumauncer.
> (*Antechrist*, in *Rom.* xxix. 80.)

From the same period :

> Si joe l'ordre des cases ne gart,
> Ne ne juigne part a sa part ;
> Certes nen dei estre reprise,
> Ke nel puis faire en nule guise.
> Qu'en latin est nominatif
> Ço frai romanz acusatif.
> Un faus franceis sai d'Angletere
> Ke nel alai ailurs quere.
> (A fragment of a *Life of Edward the Confessor*, ed. Baker, in *M. L. R.* iii. 374.)

From the end of the thirteenth century :

> De le français ne del rimer
> Ne me dait nuls hom blamer,
> Kar en Engletere fu né
> E nurri lenz e ordiné.

(Wilham de Wadington, *Manuel des pechez* ; cf. *Hist. Litt. de la France*, xxviii. 180.)

From the end of the fourteenth century :

> Poy sai latin, poy sai romance.
>
> .   .   .   .   .
>
> Et si jeo n'ai de François la faconde,
> Pardonetz moi qe jeo de ceo forsvoie :
> Jeo sui Englois, si quier par tiele voie
> Estre excusé.

(John Gower, *Mirour de l'Omme*, ed. Macaulay, pp. 246, 391.)

It is instructive to compare these utterances with similar admissions made by writers during the latter days of Latin. Gregory of Tours, for instance, says : 'Ueniam legentibus praecor si aut in litteris aut in sillabis grammaticam artem excessero, de qua adplene non sum inbutus'.... 'Saepius pro masculinis feminea, pro femineis neutra et pro neutra masculina conmutas, qui ipsas quoque praepositiones ... loco debito plerumque non locas ; nam ablatiuis accusatiua et rursum accusatiuis ablatiua praeponis' (Max Bonnet, *Le Latin de Grégoire de Tours*, p. 78 ff.).

II. THE CHARACTER OF ANGLO-NORMAN

THE French language was brought to England mainly by Normans, and the French of England originally bears the features of the Norman dialect in the form appropriate to the period at which the language was conveyed from one country to the other.   The oldest Anglo-Norman has, in common with Norman, the following features :

In Phonology :

1. *o* or *u* for *ou*, *eu* : *seignor*, *seignur* (Suchier, *Voy. ton.* 53).

2. *ei* for *oi*: *rei* (ibid. 93).

3. distinction of *an* and *en* (ibid. 128, and for the later period, Tanneberger, *Gower*, 20).

4. confusion of *ain* and *ein*, e. g. *chaeines : semaines* in *Brendan*, 865 (Suchier, 134).

5. *ie* for *e*: *trinitiet* in *Alexis* ms. L, *raachatierre* in *Cambr. Psalt.* xviii. 14; Norman *mier*, ibid. ms. P. xciv, 5, &c. (Schumann, *Vokalismus u. Kons. des Cambr. Ps.* 14; Vising, *Le Purg.* 54; according to Suchier, 43, subst. in -*ierre* (< Lat. -*ator*) even in French).

6. fall of pretonic *e*: *alures* for *aleures*, in *IV Livres des rois*, III. iv. 6–8; *ust* for *eust*, ibid. III. xii. 10, &c. (cf. Tanquerey, *L'Évol.* 497, 607 ff., 668 ff.) ; Norman *abitor* for *abiteor* (cf. *Rom.* xxv. 323).

7. *ca* (beside *cha*): *camps* in *IV Livres des rois*, IV. vii. 12 (Stimming, *Boeve*, 235); for (north) Norman see Schwan-Behrens, *Gramm.* § 139 Anm.; Gröber's *Gdr.* map ; Moisy, *Dict. de patois norm.*, p. cxxiii.

8. *ga* (beside *ja*): *goie* (*gaudia*) in *Oxf. Psalt.* xx. 6 (Stimming, *Boeve*, 237); for (north) Norman see Schwan-Behrens, 98 ; Moisy, p. cxxv.

In Morphology :

1. accusative for nominative ; cf. Menger, *A.-N. Dial.* 112.

2. -*om*, -*on* (-*um*, -*un*) for -*oms*, -*ons* in verbs: *poum* in *Brendan*, l. 397, &c.; for Norman see Schneider, *Die Verbalformen bei Wace*, 14 (Lorentz, *Die erste Pers. Pl. des Verbums*, 25, 44 ; Tanquerey, *L'Évol.* 178, 191).

Some of these traits, such as the fall of pretonic *e* and the decay of declension, are more fully developed in Anglo-Norman than on the Continent, in illustration of the fact that languages often progress more rapidly and more radically at the circumference than at the centre. This development constitutes a first mark of differentiation between Anglo-Norman and Norman.

But Anglo-Norman developed characteristics of its own. Though it is difficult to state whether some of these are due to continental influence or not, the following phenomena may be considered to be more or less characteristic of Anglo-Norman.

In Phonology :

1. *e* for *ie*, from the middle of the twelfth century : eight examples from Samson in S. Hilgers, *DerLautstand*, &c. 19 (cf. *Z. f. fr. S. u. L.* xxxix. 11).

2. confusion of *u* and *o*, of the same date : *plus : vertuus*, Gaimar's *Chron.* 1935 (cf. M. K. Pope, *Étude*, 19 ; Tanneberger, *Gower*, 31, 37).

3. confusion of *u* and *ui*, in rhymes of the second half of the twelfth century : *pertus* (for *pertuis*) : *sus* in *Tristan*, 1157, &c. ; for later examples v. Tanneberger, *Gower*, 36, 38.

4. confusion of *ei* and *ai*: *disaie* in the oldest ms. of *Cambr. Psalt.* xciii. 18, &c.; *palais* in a laisse in -*eis*, Fantosme's *Chron.* 154 (cf. Vising, *Le Purg.* 63).

5. post-tonic *i* for *e* in the ending -*is*, from the early twelfth century : *chosis* in *Oxf. Psalt.* xv. 6 ; *spinis* in *Brendan*, 1288 ; more frequent later (cf. Tanquerey,202) and probably due to English influence (cf. Kaluza, *Hist. Gramm. der engl. Sprache*, ii. 126).

6. fall of post-tonic *e* in rhymes of the second half of the twelfth century : *gravent* for *gravente* in Fantosme's *Chron.* 1785 ; *e* not counted in the interior of the verse as early as *Haveloc*, 304, 698, &c. (cf. Tanquerey, 772 ff.).

7. *aun* and *oun* for *an*, *on*, from the beginning of the thirteenth century : *enchauntement*, &c. (cf. Vising, *Jahresbericht über die Fortschritte der rom. Phil.* XII. i. 211) ; *noun*, &c. (cf. Stimming, *Boeve*, 192 ; Vising, *Le Purg.* 56 ff.).

8. *au* for *a* before *s*, late : *oraust*, &c., *Manuel des pechez*, 7830, 8694, &c.; *chaustel*, Langtoft's *Chron.* i. 139, 141, &c.

9. final *ai* retained as a diphthong ; see Tanneberger, 8 ; cf. Tanquerey, 63.

10. confusion of *ñ* and *n* from the first half of the twelfth century: *feinnent* (<*fingunt*); *peinent*, in *Brendan*, 215 (cf. Tanneberger, 40).

11. confusion of *l'* and *l*, later : *viel*, ms. of Fantosme's *Chron.* 34, &c. (cf. Tanneberger, 12, 22, 42).

12. *dl*, *dn* for *sl*, *sn*, from the second half of the twelfth century : *pedles* in *Cambr. Psalt.* cxlvii. 2 ; *adnes* in *IV Livres des Reis*, I. ix. 3, 5, &c.

13. *th* for intervocalic (seldom final) *t*, in the earliest mss.: *absoluthe*, &c. in A.-N. ms. of *Alexis* (ed. Paris, p. 93).

14. final *d* for *t*: *ad*, *fud*, ibid. 97 (cf. Stimming, *Boeve*, p. 221 ; Tanquerey, 208).

In Morphology :

1. *lu*, *lui* as definite article, from the times of Angier (1212 ; cf. Vising, *Le Purg.*, p. 56).

2. fall of *s* in adjectives (and article) before substantive, late : *orrible tormentz* (ibid., p. 11).

3. transference to the conjugation in *-er*, from the middle of the twelfth century : *combaté : regné*, Gaimar's *Chron.* 1797 (ibid., p. 54, and Tanquerey, 392 ff., 478 ff., 560 ff., 577 ff.).

4. sigmatic perfects: *vist*, *oïst*, late (cf. Vising, op. cit., p. 12 ; Tanneberger, *Gower*, 45 ; Tanquerey, 114).

5. ending *-mus* for *-mes*: *sumus*, *veomus*, late (cf. Tanquerey, 168 ; Vising, *Deux Poèmes de Bozon*, p. xv ; Maitland, p. xli, explains *-mus* as a misexpansion of the compendium m^9).

6. ending *-et* for *-ez*: *pernet*, &c. (cf. Tanquerey and Stimming, op. cit. 230).

7. ending *-int* for *-ent* : *avindrint* (cf. Tanquerey, 257 ; Vising, *Le Purg.* 69).

8. substitution of forms of the subjunctive for forms of the indicative: *suvienge* for *suvient*, &c., late (cf. Tanquerey, 280, 805 ; Vising, *Deux Poèmes*, p. xv).

In Syntax :

1. use of tonic, instead of atonic, personal pronouns, from the first half of the twelfth century : *chi lui requerent* in *Oxf. Psalt.* xxi. 28 (cf. Vising, *Le Purg.* p. 55).

2. confusion of *tu* and *vous*, late : *tu faistes*, Langtoft's *Chron.* i. 114 (cf. Menger, *The A.-N. Dial.* 115).

3. use of imperfect as perfect, from Angier (cf. an observation of Paul Meyer, *Rom.* xii. 200) ; later examples in *Cron. de London* (ed. Aungier) : *robberent et ardoyent*, p. 45, &c. ; for misuse of perfect see Maitland, p. lxi.

4. future and conditional after *si*, e.g. Fantosme's *Chron.*: *si ja m'orrez mentir*, v. 1152, &c. ; *si home serreit receu* in *Year Books of Edw. II*, Introduction, lxxiii.

5. *aveir* with intransitive and reflexive verbs, from the second part of the twelfth century : *venue a ma plaie guarir* in *Tristan*, 2560 ; *s'en ad iree*, ibid. 933 ; *il se ad dit rey*, in *Ev. Nicod.* 499. (This is rare on the Continent.)

6. accusative after intransitive verbs with *estre*, late : *est la vile entrez*, Langtoft's *Chron.* i. 304, &c.

7. *de* instead of *pour*, late : *est ore au boys alé d'eplucher noiz* (Bozon, *Plainte d'Amour*, 678 ; see ed., commentaire, p. 15).

Some syntactical phenomena considered by Ernst Burghardt (*Einfluss des Engl. auf das Anglon.*, p. 23 ff.) to be borrowed from English are not exclusively A.-N.

In Orthography :

1. *eo* (*u, e*) for *ue* : *eovre* in the oldest ms. of *Cambr. Psalt.* xvi. 4 (cf. Suchier, *Voy. ton.* 98 ff.; Tanneberger, 29 ; Vising, *Le Purg.* 55) ; [*oe* for *eu* in pron. *icoels*, *Oxford Psalt.* (2) v. 9, ix. 5, 6, &c.].

2. *aa, ee* (seldom *oo, ii*), late : *paas* in *Dist. Catonis*, *Anon.* (ed. Stengel), l. 277, Langtoft's *Chron.* ii. 332 ; *eestre*, *Rom.* xv, p. 317 ; *pees*, Langtoft's *Chron.* ii. 132, Vising, *Le Purg.* p. 11 ; *equitee*, Bozon, *Contes*, 10, 23, 25, &c. (isolated in earlier mss.) ; *cool, oos*, Walter de Bibbesworth (ed. Wright), pp. 146, 149 ; *mespriis, diist, Rom.* xxxii. 32, 33.

For other orthographic peculiarities see Maitland, p. xlii ff.

In Vocabulary :

1. words of Latin origin, as : *cester, chinche[sce], contek, courtehours, denaturesce, eindegree, ennoyter, naturesce, travanter* ; see the Glossaries of Bozon's *Contes, Plainte d'Amour, Deux Poèmes.*

2. words of English origin, as *englemure, framure, gilerie, [h]udivesce, wibet, wivre, wodecoke* ; cf. ibid. and W. W. Skeat, *A Rough List* and *A Second List.*

3. peculiar forms of words, as *chescun, dount* (for *donc*), *unquore* (cf. above-cited Glossaries) ; *solum, oveske* (cf. Vising, *Le Purg.* Glossary).

These and other less important characteristics sufficiently distinguish A.-N. from continental French dialects. They appear unequally not only, as has been indicated, at different periods, but also in works of the same period; in some works very few of them are found.

It is necessary also to take account of the features borrowed by Anglo-Norman from other French dialects, as a consequence of the immigrations from south-western France under the Angevins and later of the settlement of a great many monks, soldiers, and tradesmen from northern France, and the intercourse of the nobility and the learned with Paris and its university. So we have in A.-N. the traits that seem to indicate south-western origin :

1. *-aige* for *-age*, from the second half of the fourteenth century : *homaiges* (cf. Busch, *Laut- und Formenlehre der anglon. Sprache*, 12 ; Goerlich, *Die südwestl. Dial.* 35).

2. *eie* for *ee*, as early as *Cambr. Psalt.*: *sudeiement*,lxiii. 4 (cf. Goerlich, 18).

3. *eus* for *eaus*, from the end of the twelfth century : *guasteus*, Cott. ms. of *Brendan*, 410 ; *oiseus*, ibid. 499 (cf. Goerlich, 54 ff.).

4. *i* for pretonic *e* after *ch* in mss. of the thirteenth century : *chivaler*, Gaimar's *Chron.* (ms. 127, 2734, etc., Goerlich, 74); even other influences from the same region are assumed by Miss Pope in her *Étude sur la langue de Frère Angier*, passim.

Several cases of influence from the Walloon and Picard dialects on the verbal forms are assumed by Tanquerey in *L'Évol.* 854.

Some later traits in A.-N., as *an* for *en*, *oi* for *ei* (*roi*), *s* for *c* (*siel*, &c., cf. Vising, *Le Purg.* 11), *-eie* for *-oue* in the first conjugation, &c., are common to most of the French dialects, and may have been introduced from the south-west or the centre of France or from any other region to which they belong.

It is difficult to fix distinct periods for the evolution of Anglo-Norman. The individualism of the authors is too great, and their command of the language too unequal. It seems, however, that about a hundred years after the Conquest a decided differentiation from the original language had set in. We find plain evidence of it in Fantosme's *Chronicle*. There, more clearly than before, we find *e* rhyming with *ie* (Vising, *Étude*, 92), *ai* confused with *ei*, atonic *e* neglected, the future in conditional sentences, the rules of declension disregarded, and the versification disorganized. Moreover, we find in Fantosme the adoption from southern France of the ending *-aire* for Lat. *-ator* (*-ater*), rhyming with *paire* (Lat. *pater*), *depuignaire* (Lat. *depugnator*), *fraire*, &c., with *faire*, *contraire*, &c. (laisse ii); but this is an individual trait.

During the thirteenth century Anglo-Norman became more and more inconsistent and irregular, and we have seen that many authors confess their uncertain knowledge of the language. The linguistic phenomena are in that century very difficult to date, but about a hundred years after Fantosme a new epoch may be said to have begun. We then often find *au* before *s*, the definite article *lu, lui*, sigmatic perfects, the ending *-mus, -et* for *-ez, -int* for *-ent*, subjunctive forms for indicative, *tu* confounded with *vous*, the accusative after intransitive verbs, and specialized forms of French words adopted from English. It is noteworthy that official Anglo-Norman, which begins at a late date, in legal documents, reports of cases, &c., is in its irregularities fairly consistent and preserves a certain tradition.

I. GENERAL OUTLINE

A RAPID glance at Anglo-Norman literature will show us that this literature is mainly religious and didactic or practical. Such was also the literature of the Normans. This is a natural consequence of the general Norman character, which Gaston Paris has strikingly sketched in *La Littérature normande avant l'annexion.* ‘C’est qu’en effet l’esprit normand n’a rien de langoureux, pas plus qu’il n’a rien de chimérique, rien de mystique ou de romanesque. Ce qui le caractérise avant tout, c’est l’ordre, la clarté, la raison aiguisée d’esprit, avec un certain réalisme et positivisme.’ And again : ‘Un autre trait du caractère normand d’alors qui se reflète dans la littérature est la dévotion, non pas une dévotion exaltée et mystique, mais une dévotion profonde, sincère et riche en œuvres.’ These traits are at once recognizable in those who founded the Anglo-Norman régime in England, and they have set their stamp upon the literature.

The biblical literature is comparatively rich, and it includes some very valuable texts, such as the two oldest translations of the Psalter. Legends of saints and sermons also exist in numerous texts, and Anglo-Norman lyric poetry is almost exclusively religious. It is a remarkable fact that there are two very interesting specimens of the religious drama in England before we have any monuments of the drama in France.

It is true that a great deal of the religious literature consists in translation from Latin originals, but literary activity was during the Middle Ages often nothing but translation or adaptation, and this activity was often held in as high esteem as original creation. In many instances the Latin originals themselves derive from Anglo-Norman sources, and thus have a twofold importance for Anglo-Norman literature.

Of didactic and utilitarian literature there are two classes which had a very extensive vogue : the chronicle, and official and legal documents and treatises.

The taste for historical works is especially characteristic of the Anglo-Normans. This has been forcibly pointed out by Professor Lewis Jones in *The Cambridge History of English Literature*. 'Of all the literary monuments', he says, ' of the remarkable revival of learning which followed the coming of the Normans, and which reached its zenith under Henry II, the greatest, alike in bulk and in permanent interest and value, is the voluminous mass of Latin chronicles compiled during the twelfth and the thirteenth centuries. So ample is the wealth of this chronicle literature, and so full and trustworthy is its presentment of contemporary affairs, that few periods in our history stand out in such clear and minute relief as that of the Norman and Angevin kings' (vol. i, p. 156). What is said here of the Latin chroniclers may be said with almost equal truth of the Anglo-Norman chroniclers. Professor Lewis Jones continues : ' No other country produced, during the twelfth and the thirteenth centuries, anything to be compared with the English chronicles in variety of interest, wealth of information, and amplitude of range. So wide is their outlook, and so authoritative is their record of events, that, as Stubbs observes, it is from the English chroniclers of this period that much of the German history of the time has to be written ' (ibid.). The oldest chronicle in Anglo-Norman is that of Geffrey Gaimar. It is true that it is not original, but it is the first chronicle in the French language. The next chronicle in order of date, that of Jordan Fantosme, is entirely original.

The official and legal literature is so extensive and the bulk of documents relating to official life is so great that it has been said that only an enthusiast can think of publishing the whole of it (Pike in *Year Books of Edward III*, anno xiv, p. xiv).

In all this, however, we see the mark of the Anglo-Norman character, as we do also in the fact that lyric poetry, other than religious, hardly exists in Anglo-Norman literature. It must be acknowledged that the scanty poems on love and other lyrical subjects cited in ch. iii, B, § 3, and ch. iv, B, § 1, are very poor as literary productions, with the possible exception of nos. 359 a, 360, whose authors had learnt their art in France.

In one respect Anglo-Norman literature is much superior to Norman literature, namely, in narrative poetry. As is shown in ch. ii, B, § 1, and ch. iii, B, § 1, Anglo-Norman literature can boast a great number of romances, some of which have a very high literary value. *Horn*, *Tristan*, the romances by Hue de Rotelande and others, are among the finest works of their kind. In them new elements—Celtic, Anglo-Saxon, or Scandinavian traditions — were superposed on an original Norman basis.

The greater part of Anglo-Norman literature is anonymous, and in this respect resembles mediaeval literature in general. In many cases where the authors have told us their names we know nothing or next to nothing about them. The best of them, such as the Thomas who wrote *Horn*, and the Thomas who is the author of *Tristan*, are otherwise completely unknown to us. Philipe de Thaun wrote four poems of considerable extent, but all we know about him is that he was a cleric living in the first half of the twelfth century. Nicholas Bozon is the author of a great number of works, but we are reduced to mere conjecture about the time and the region to which he belongs.

When men of high estate occupy themselves with poetry, they commonly add little to their glory. So it was when the illustrious bishop Robert Grosseteste wrote his *Chasteau d'amour*; and when Henry de Lacy and Walter de Bibbesworth attempted to compose a tenzon the result was somewhat ludicrous (no. 237).

It is among men of the Church that most of the literary authors are to be found. Even a writer of romances, the author of *Horn*, is evidently a cleric, as is also the chief Anglo-Norman writer of works on natural science, Philipe de Thaun.

It is to the credit of the clergy that they were most diligent in copying literary works, and in this way have preserved to us not only the works of their countrymen but also many continental works of great value, as the oldest text of *Roland*, the *Chançun de Guillaume*, the *Pèlerinage de Charlemagne*, the *Vie de Guillaume le Maréchal*, *L'Estoire de la Guerre sainte* by Ambroise, *La Destruction de Rome*, &c.

The following catalogue of Anglo-Norman literature is arranged in chronological order, so as to give a general survey of the productions of the different centuries. It is true that the dating of a great many works is very uncertain, especially of small pieces and in general of the works of the thirteenth century. But an approximate date can be arrived at in most instances.

Thus it immediately appears that the great religious literature, the most valuable translations of biblical books, as well as the great epic literature, belong to the twelfth century; that the smaller pieces, including sermons, are very numerous in the thirteenth century; that didactic and practical literature, such as works on natural science, philological works, laws and public documents, belong principally to the thirteenth and fourteenth centuries, and that, except for official documents and some very few works of other kinds, Anglo-Norman literature comes to an end in the fifteenth century. The last considerable representative of this literature is John Gower (†1408), equally famous as an English and a Latin poet.

The law literature of the sixteenth to eighteenth centuries forms a chapter apart.

Concerning the locality to which Anglo-Norman works belong it is in most cases impossible to state anything with certainty. It is possible, however, to make certain inferences, with the following results:

HAMPSHIRE (Southampton and Winchester): Elie's *Disticha Catonis* (44), Guischart's *Sermon* (22), and probably *Horn* (see Hartenstein, p. 28) in the twelfth century; *On Unchastity* (256; cf. the end of the poem) in the thirteenth century; *The Oak Book* (395) and a number of official writings of a later date.

KENT: *Alexander* (37) in the twelfth century; Rauf's

Calendar (303), Peckham's *Lumière* (157), and *Secret des Secrets* (250) in the thirteenth century; and Gower's *Poems* in the fourteenth century.

LONDON (Westminster, Barking): Clemence's *Catherine* (11), Adgar's *Legends* (13, Prol. l. 40), Fantosme's *Chronicle* (62) in the twelfth century; *Edward the Confessor* (125; see Fritz, p. 125), *La Riote* (268, l. 5, &c.) in the thirteenth century; and most of the official Documents.

OXFORD: Angier's *S. Gregory* (108) in the thirteenth century, and Trevet's *Chronicle* (379) in the fourteenth century.

HERTFORDSHIRE: Borron's *Graal* (36) in the twelfth century; *S. Alban* (115) and Walter de Bibbesworth's works (160, 237, 386) in the thirteenth century. Possibly Benet's *Thomas* (19; cf. *Literaturbl. f. g. u. r. Phil.* 1888, p. 177).

SUFFOLK: Grosseteste's works (153, 328), Everard de Gateley's *Miracles* (98), and probably the poem no. 93, in the thirteenth century.

NORTHAMPTON, RUTLAND: *Guy of Warwick* (212) and possibly Gretham's *Miroir* (71) in the thirteenth century; *Scalacronica* (382) in the fourteenth century.

HEREFORD: Simund de Freine's *Poems* (16, 55), Hue de Rotelande's *Romances* (32, 33), and Adam de Ross's *S. Paul* (17) in the twelfth century.

LINCOLNSHIRE: Samson de Nantuil's *Proverbs* (4) in the twelfth century; Henry d'Arcy's *Poems* (111–14), *Hugo of Lincoln* (223), and Wadington's *Manuel* (158) in the thirteenth century.

YORKSHIRE: Gaimar's *Chronicle* (61) in the twelfth century; Langtoft's *Chronicle* (377) in the fourteenth century. Bozon also was presumably connected with this region; cf. edition of no. 291, p. ix.

WALES: Simon de Kernethin's *Sermon* (149) in the thirteenth century.

II–VI. DETAILED CATALOGUE OF WORKS

II. THE TWELFTH CENTURY

A. Religious Literature

§ I. THE BIBLE

1. *Oxford* (or *Montebourg*) *Psalter.* Early XII.—(1) Francisque Michel, *Libri Psalmorum versio antiqua gallica.* Oxford, 1860. (2) Beyer in *Z. f. rom. Ph.* xi. 513 ff., xii. 1 ff. (Ps. iv–liv from ms. *94*).—*37, 87, 94, 165* (early XII. according to Madan, late XII. according to Michel), *242, 381, 387.* Later mss. with or without glosses, as *60, 76, 250* (cf. Surtees Soc. 1843–4), differ more or less and may be considered new versions.—Berger, *La Bible*, 10; Delisle, *Not. et Extr.* XXXIV. i. 259; Meister, *Die Flexion im O. Ps.* (1879); Harseim, *Vocalismus u. Cons. im O. Ps.* (1879); Varnhagen, *Das C im O. Ps.* (*Z. f. rom. Ph.* iii); Gorges, *Über Stil u. Ausdruck einiger altfr. Prosaübers.* (1882); Suchier in *Z. f. rom. Ph.* viii. 416.—French Psalters down to the XVIth century are for the most part reproductions of this Psalter, giving the Gallican text with literal renderings; see Berger, p. 200; P. Meyer, *Ro.* xvii. 124; Suchier; Margarete Förster, *Die franz. Psalmenübers.* (1914) I.

2. *Cambridge* (or *Canterbury*) *Psalter.* Early XII.—Francisque Michel, *Le Livre des Psaumes*, Paris, 1886.—*300* (incomplete; written by Eadmund about 1160), *386.*—Berger, *La Bible*, 1; Dreyer, *Die Flexion im C. Ps.* (1879); Dreyer, *Der Lautstand im C. Ps.* (1882); Schumann, *Vokalismus u. Kons. des C. Ps.* (1883); Suchier, *Z. f. rom. Ph.* viii. 416; M. Förster, op. cit., 8.—This translation is based on Jerome's version from the Hebrew.

3. *Canticles, Creeds,* &c. Early XII.—Francisque Michel in *Libri Psalm. vers. ant.*, 232; *Le Livre des Psaumes*, 263.— Most of the oldest mss. of the Psalters. See Berger, 19.

4. *Proverbs of Solomon* with glosses, 11,854 ll. by SAMSON DE NANTUIL. *c.* 1140.—Extr. (1) Th. Wright, *Biographia Brit. Lit.*, A.-N. Par. 130; (2) Bartsch-Horning, *Langue et Litt. fr.* 149.—*82* (v. Gabrielson, *Sermons de Guischart de Beauliu*, 1).—Hedvig Hilgers, *Die Wortstellung in S. d. N.* (1910); Sophie Hilgers, *Der Lautstand in den Prov. von S. d. N.* (1910); Suchier, *Gesch. d. fr. Lit.* i. 118.—

☞ The following order is observed in this catalogue:—No. of piece, name of piece and its author (where known), short description of its character and form, date (*c.* = *circa* ; twelfth century is abbreviated as XII.).—Editions in whole or part (Extr. = Extracts).—Nos. of MSS. in italics referring to List, ch. viii, pp. 88 ff.—References to dissertations, articles, notes, &c., on the piece.

42 **Anglo-Norman Literature**

Samson wrote for Lady Aaliz de Cundé, of Horncastle, Lincolnshire.
The text of the Proverbs ends in the 19th chapter. The glosses are
based upon various Latin commentaries. The style is agreeable and
the work cleverly done.

5. *Li IV Livre des Reis*, prose translation, but occasionally rhymed.
c. 1170 (with traces of an earlier version).—(1) Leroux de Lincy, 1841 ;
(2) Curtius, 1911 (for the Gesellsch. f. rom. Lit.).—*353, 372, 389, 390,
394.*—Curtius, and special works cited by him p. xiii, to which add
Köhler, *Syntakt. Untersuch. über* ... (1888).—This translation is, according to G. Paris, ' œuvre d'une haute valeur, faite avec une singulière in-
telligence et une liberté qui n'exclut pas la fidélité, et qui nous offre un
excellent spécimen de notre langue à l'une de ses meilleures époques'
(*Litt. norm. avant l'annexion*, 36.) Paris believed, as many others,
that this translation was Norman ; but it was probably executed in
England ; cf. Curtius, pp. lxxxviii–xcv. The oldest and best ms. (*390*)
is evidently A.-N.

6. *Metrical Psalter*, 2460 six-line stanzas. End of XII.—Extr.
by (1) P. Meyer in *Jahrb. f. r. e. L.* (1866), 37 ; (2) Bonnard, *Les Traductions de la Bible en vers*, 130 ; (3) Goedicke, *Über d. anglon.
Schweifreimpsalter* (1910), 33.—*81, 94* (fragm.), *324.*—Goedicke ;
Inc. 57.

7. *Commentary on the Psalter*. End of XII.—Extr. (1) P. Meyer,
Docum. manuscr. 89 ; (2) Berger, *La Bible*, 65.—*18, 310.*—' Il paraît
être à peu près exactement traduit ou du moins imité de celui de saint
Augustin ' (Berger).

8. *History of Mary and Jesus*, fragment of 210 ll. *c.* 1200.—
P. Meyer, *Ro.* xvi. 253.—*42.*

9. *Stories from the Bible*, about 4,500 ll. *c.* 1200.—Extr. (1) Baker,
Die versifizierte Übers. der fr. Bibel in Hds. Egerton, 2710 (1897) ;
(2) *Ro.* xvi. 182 ; (3) *Bull. Soc. a. t.* (1889), 74 ; (4) *Not. et Extr.* XXXIV.
i. 210.—*121, 188, 304, 347, 348, 376, 415* ; *304, 376, 415* are fragmentary ; the others end at Kings iv.—These biblical stories, based
on the Vulgate and Jerome's Commentaries, are rendered into prose in
two mss. (Berger, *La Bible*, 54, 350), one of which has A.-N. features.
See also Andresen, *Eine altfr. Bearbeitung bibl. Stoffe*, 1916. Another
prose version of a biblical poem on the *Genesis and Exodus* is quoted
by P. Meyer, *Ro.* xvii. 140 ; ms. *78.*

§ 2. SAINTS' LIVES

10. *Brendan's Voyage*, 1834 ll. by BENEEIT. *c.* 1122.—(1) Suchier
in *Rom. Stud.* i (mss. *45, 179*); F. Michel, *Les Voyages merveilleux
de S. B.* (1878 ; ms. *374*) ; (2) Auracher in *Z. f. rom. Ph.* ii (ms. *388*).
A new ed. from all the mss. is in preparation by E. G. R. Waters.—
45, 179, 318, 374, 388.—Vising, *Étude sur le dial. anglo-n.* (1882) ;
Birkenhoff, *Über Metrum u. Reim d. altfr. Brandanleg.* (1884) ; Ham-
mer, *Die Sprache* ... in *Z. f. rom. Ph.* ix (1885) ; Brekke, *Étude sur
la flexion dans* ... (1885) ; Wien, *Das Verhältn. der Handschr.* (1886) ;
Wahlund, *Brendans Meerfahrt* (Upsala, 1900 ; bibliography, pp.
lxxxvi ff.) ; Calmund, *Prolegomena zu einer Ausgabe des* ... (1902 ;

review in *Jahresb. rom. Ph.* vii).—Dedicated to Queen Alice, wife of Henry II.—The source is probably a Latin *Navigatio S. Brendani,* not the *Vita Brendani* in MS. Bodl. e Mus. 3 (*Zeitschr. f. celt. Phil.* v. 1 ; cf. *Vitae Sanctorum Hiberniae,* i, p. xlii ; and Pfitzner, *Das anglon. Gedicht von Br.* 1910, 36).—Cf. Schulze in *Z. f. rom. Ph.* xxx. 257.

11. *Catherine of Alexandria,* 2688 ll. by CLEMENCE OF BARKING, a nun. *c.* 1150-60.—Jarnik, *Dve verse starofrancouské legende o sv. Katerine alexandrinské.* Prague, 1894.—*330, 366, 374.*—Knust, *Gesch. d. h. Katharina von Alex. u. d. h. Maria Aeg.* (1890) ; Mussàfia in *Zeitschr. f. d. österr. Gymn.* (1896); Manger, *Die franz. Bearb. d. Leg. d. h. K. von A.* (1901); Hilka, *Arch. n. Spr.* cxl. 171. Clemence declares herself (l. 32) that she is translating a Latin original, for which v. Manger, 4.

12. *La Passiun de seint Edmund,* 424 four-line stanzas. 1150-60.— Nabert, 1915 ; Extr. in *Ro.* xxxvi. 533 (P. Meyer).—*260.*—Principal source Abbo of Fleury, *Passio Sancti Eadmundi* (Nabert, 9).

13. *49 Miracles of Mary of Egypt* (and a few other saints) by WILLAME ADGAR ; the legends vary in length from 18 to 1100 ll. *c.* 1160-70.—(1) Neuhaus, *Adgars Marienlegenden* (1886 ; 40 Miracles from ms. *117* ; no. 40 is probably not by Adgar) ; (2) Herbert in *Ro.* xxxii. (nine Miracles from ms. *116,* and *De l'abesse enceintée* from ms. *117).* For other partial editions, see Neuhaus, iii ; Herbert, 396.— *116* (22 Miracles, often abridged), *117* (incomplete), *323* (fragment).— Rolfs, *Die Adgariegenden Egerton 612* in *Rom. Forsch.* i. (1883) ; Ward, *Catal.* ii. 708 ; Vising, *Jahresb. rom. Ph.* VII. ii. 88. The sources of Adgar's poems are chiefly *Miracula Dei genitricis* by William of Malmesbury ; partly Ildefonsus of Toledo. Cf. Mussafia, *Stud. zu d. mittelalt. Marienleg.* (Vienna Acad., 1887 seq.).

14. *La Vie seint Edmund le Rei,* 4032 ll. by DENIS PIRAMUS. *c.* 1170-80.—(1) Arnold in *Memorials of St. Edmund's Abbey* (Rolls, 1892) ; (2) F. L. Ravenel in *Bryn Mawr Coll. Monographs* (1906) ; (3) Lord Fr. Hervey in *Corolla S. Eadmundi* (1907).—*51.*—Haxo in *Mod. Phil.* xii. 345, 559 (also as Dissertation). The author says : ' Translaté l'ai desque a la fin | E del engleis e del latin ' (l. 3268) ; these English and Latin sources have been indicated by Haxo, who also tries to show that Denis Piramus is identical with a Magister Dionisius, of whom mention is made in Jocelin's *Chronicles* from the year 1173 to 1202. Denis is considered by Haxo to be of continental extraction, possibly from Maine.

15. *Vie de S. Gilles,* 3794 ll. by GUILLAUME DE BERNEVILLE. 2nd half of XII.—(1) G. Paris and Bos (Soc. a. t., 1881) ; (2) Brandin.—*70* (fragm. ed. Brandin, *Ro.* xxxiii. 94), *404.*—The author says that he is a ' chanoine Ki s'est peiné e travaillé De ceste vie translater ' (l. 3761). He has, however, translated his original, *Vita S. Egidii,* freely.

16. *Vie de S. Georges,* 1711 ll. by SIMUND DE FREINE (named in the acrostic opening of the poem). Late XII.—Matzke (Soc. a. t., 1909).— *348.*—The principal source is a Latin *Vita* (see ed., p. lxxxvii). The author was a canon of Hereford and friend of Giraldus Cambrensis.

17. *The Vision of S. Paul,* 421 ll. by ADAM DE ROSS. End of XII.—

Kastner in *Z. f. fr. S. u. L.* xxix. 274.—*44, 166, 255, 260, 364.* (Cf. *Jahresb. rom. Ph.* x. ii. 109.)—Adam's source is a *Vita S. Pauli Apostoli*, ed. P. Meyer, *Ro.* xxiv. 364.

18. *Vie de S. Marguerite*, 67 six-line stanzas. *c.* 1200.—(1) Spencer, Leipzig, 1889 ; (2) Extr. *Ro.* xv. 268.—*220.—Ro.* xix. 477, where P. Meyer doubts if this poem is A.-N. *Hist. littér.* xxxiii. 362. For the Latin source, see ed., p. 46.

19. *Thomas of Canterbury*, 353 six-line stanzas by BENET (l. 1427), *c.* 1185 (Walberg, *Ro.* xliv. 407).—Francisque Michel in *Chroniques des Ducs de Normandie* iii. 416, 619.—*46, 47, 79, 242* (not Kk. 48 as in *Hist. Litt.* xxxiii. 377), *305, 348.*—Benet, a monk of St. Albans, translated a Latin original (l. 1430).

20, 21. *Barlaam and Josaphat*, 2954 ll., and *Seven Sleepers*, 1898 ll. by CHARDRY. *c.* 1200.—Koch in *Chardry's Josaphaz, Set Dormanz und Petit Plet* (Altfranz. Bibl., 1879). Cf. no. 56.—*33, 196.*—The Latin originals have not been identified with certainty ; cf. Gröber in *Grundriss,* II. i. 643 ; Mussafia in *Z. f. rom. Ph.* iii. 591 ; Schofield, 118.

Note. *La Vie de S. Marie l'Egyptienne*, publ. by A. T. Baker in *Rev. d. l. r.* lix, is doubtfully A.-N., though it has been regarded as such both by myself (*Versification anglo-n.* 75) and by its recent editor. It is rather Norman. The *Miracle de Sardenai* also, which I regarded formerly as A.-N. (op. cit., p. 74), seems to me now to belong to continental Norman, though most of the mss. are A.-N. (*3, 194, 236, 399*).

A collection of Miracles made, or at least copied, in England, and existing in fragments in a ms. at Orléans, is hardly A.-N. The language, even in the declensions and the versification, is so regular that there is every probability that they are continental in origin, though Gröber classes them as Anglo-French (*Gdr.* II. i. 649). P. Meyer has published the fragments of the Orléans ms. in *Not. et Extr.* XXXIV. ii. 47. They are partly based on Gregory's Dialogues, like the three Miracles in the ms. Camb. Pembr. Coll. 258 (ms. *274*) : ' Seynt Gregorie pape de Rome ', which is of doubtful provenance (cf. M. R. James's *Catal.*).

A.-N. prose legends are very rare. In P. Meyer's list, *Hist. littér.* xxxiii, there are none. The few A.-N. mss. that contain prose legends are copies of French originals (cf. ibid., 397), for the reason that this class of literature did not come into vogue until A.-N. literature was in its decline, and it appealed to a more cultivated class than the metrical legends (ibid., *378*).

§ 3. SERMONS AND RELIGIOUS TREATISES

22. *Entendez ca vers moi*, sermon of 1,923 ll. in 40 laisses by GUIS-CHART DE BEAULIU. End of XII.—Gabrielson in *Sermon en vers de G. d. B.* Upsala, 1909.—*82, 121, 364.*—Gabrielson, *G. de B.'s debt to religious learning and liter. in England*, in *Arch. n. Spr.* cxxviii. 309. Beauliu is probably Beaulieu in Hampshire. Guischart is a comparatively independent poet. His sources or models seem to be Ælfric, *Poema morale, Alexis*, the sermon *Grant mal fist Adam*, and a (French ?) version of the *Debate between the body and the soul.*

23. *Deu le omnipotent*, sermon of 122 six-line stanzas. End of XII. Suchier in *Reimpredigt* (Bibl. Norm.), 82.—*86, 97, 255.*

24. *Deus nus promet*, fragment of a metrical sermon. End of XII.— Stengel in *Ausg. u. Abh.* i. 173.—*179.*

25. *Li Romanz des Romanz*, 257 four-line stanzas on the Church and Christian life. End of XII.—Extr., *Ro.* xxxii. 104 ; ed. Tanquerey, 1922.—*25, 117, 163, 242* (single complete), *282, 364, 370.* The A.-N. character of this poem is barely apparent, but all the mss., including the two Paris mss. (*364, 370*), were executed in England.

26. *The Rule of S. Benedict*, prose transl. End of XII.—Mentioned in *Libri Psalmorum,* p. x (see no. 1 above).—Berger, *La Bible,* 412. —*165.*—Later redaction in ms. Cott. Nero D. i (cf. Dugdale, *Monasticon* iii. 365).

§ 4. DRAMA

27. *Le Mystère d'Adam*, 942 ll. (end wanting). *c.* 1150–60.— P. Studer, Manchester Univ. Press, 1918 (where see pp. 59 ff. for former editions).—*400.*—P. Meyer, *Ro.* xxxii. 637, proposes an earlier date and France as the place of composition ; Vising, *Jahresb. rom. Ph.* XI. i. 250, ii. 111 ; Cohen, *Gesch. d. Inszenierung d. geistl. Schauspiele* (1907), 47. The chief source, besides the Bible, is the Pseudo-Augustinian *Sermo contra Judaeos* (v. ed., pp. xii ff.).

28. *The Resurrection of Christ*, 366 ll. (fragm.). End of XII.— (1) Jubinal, *La Résurrection du Sauveur*, Paris, 1834 ; (2) Monmerqué and Michel in *Théâtre français du moyen-âge,* 1839 ; (3) Foerster and Koschwitz in *Altfranz. Übungsbuch,* 213.—*348.*

B. Secular Literature

§ 1. ROMANCES

(On A.-N. romances see Dr. Anna Hunt Billings, *Guide to the Middle English Metrical Romances,* N.Y., 1901.)

29. *Amadas and Idoine*, fragm. of 286 ll. *c.* 1160.—Andresen in *Z. f. rom. Ph.* xiii. 87.—*411.*—G. Paris in *Engl. Misc. presented to Dr. Furnivall* (1901), 386 ; Foerster in *Z. f. rom. Ph.* xxxviii. 108. This is the original of the Picard redaction published by Hippeau in 1863.

30. *Tristan*, 3,144 ll. by THOMAS (not the author of *Horn*). *c.* 1170. —Bédier (Soc. a. t., 1902–5).—Mss. all fragmentary, *167, 215, 410,* and the lost Sneyd (XII.) and Strassburg (XIII.).—Bédier gives as the source of Thomas's *Tristan* an 'archétype', based on old Celtic tales and amplified by Thomas (as by other poets). Some traits, for instance, are borrowed from Breri and Wace. 'Cependant, par la puissance et la finesse de sa sensibilité, par les ressources de son style, par la qualité de son émotion, Thomas est un poète, remarquable entre les poètes de son temps' (ed. ii. 318).—G. Paris considered Thomas to be a Norman, and so did the present author in a pamphlet of 1902 : see *Jahresb. rom. Ph.* VI. ii. 111. For bibliographical notes see ed. ii. 41 seq.—Béroul s *Tristan* is probably continental, perhaps from Brittany.

31. *Horn,* 5,250 ll. in 245 laisses by MESTRE THOMAS (not the author of 30). *c.* 1180.—(1) Francisque Michel (for the Bannatyne Club, 1845) ; (2) Brede and Stengel in *Ausg. u. Abh.* viii (1883) ; a new edition in preparation by Miss M. K. Pope.—Mss., all incomplete, *64, 161, 225* ; and two small fragments recently discovered by Prof. Braunholtz of Cambridge (v. *M.L.R.* Jan. 1921), and now University Library MS. Addit. 4407, 4470 (*301*).—Bibliographical information in Hartenstein, *Stud. zur Hornsage,* 1902 ; Vising, *Jahresb. rom. Ph.* vii. 86, 89, and *Stud. i den fr. Rom. om Horn,* Göteborg, 1903–5 ; Schofield, *The Story of H. and Rimenhild* (*Publ. Mod. Lang. Ass.*) xviii (1903 ; cf. *Ro.* xxxiv. 147 ; *Jahresb. rom. Ph.* VII. ii. 89); Deutschbein, *Stud. zur Sagengeschichte Englands,* i (1906); Dahms, *Der Formenbau des Nom. u. Verb.* (1906); Heuser in *Anglia,* xxxi. 105. Mestre Thomas was a remarkable poet, who seems to have availed himself of Norse sagas (cf. Hartenstein, Schofield, and Deutschbein in *Anglia, Beiblatt,* 1909, p. 55). He tells us in his first lines that he has written a romance of *Aaluf,* Horn's father, a work which is totally lost, as is also an old version of *Horn* in assonances (cf. no. 215).

32. *Ipomedon,* 10,578 ll. by HUE DE ROTELANDE. *c.* 1185.—Kölbing and Koschwitz (1889).—*44, 120, 179.*—Mussafia in *Sitzungsber. der Ak. in Wien,* cxxi. 13.—Carter in *Haverford Essays* (1909), 237 (cf. *Jahresb. rom. Ph.* XII. ii. 140); Ward, *Catal.* i. 728, where it is stated that Hue lived at Credenhill, near Hereford ; Hahn, *Der Wortschatz des Dichters H. de R.* (1910). Hue took Chrétien de Troyes for his model. *Ipomedon* is especially reminiscent of *Erec,* as also of the *Rom. de Troie* and other romances (*Jahresb. rom. Ph.,* loc. cit.).

33. *Protheselaüs,* nearly 12,700 ll. by HUE DE ROTELANDE. Shortly after *Ipomedon.*—Extr. in Ward, *Catal.* i. 751 ; Kluckow, *Sprachl. u. textkrit. Stud. über Pr.* (Greifswald, 1909) ; Boenigk, *Literaturhist. Unters. zum Pr.* (Greifsw., 1909).—*120, 179, 351.*—The principal sources are Chrétien's Arthurian romances.

34. *La Folie Tristan,* 998 ll. End of XII.—(1) Francisque Michel in *Tristan,* 1835 ; (2) Bédier (Soc. a. t., 1907).—*167.*—Curdy, *La folie T.* (Dissert., Baltimore, 1903). Based on Thomas's *Tristan,* according to Bédier ; still more on Béroul's *Tristan,* according to Hoepffner, *Z. f. Ph.* xxxix. 62, 551, 672.

35. *Amis and Amiloun,* 1,250 ll. End of XII.—Kölbing in *Altengl. Bibl.* ii (1884).—*7, 244, 413.*—Link, *Eine sprachl. Stud. üb. d. anglon. Version der Amis-Sage,* 1885 ; Ward, *Catal.* i. 674. The source is the Latin legend of A. et A.

36. *Estoire du saint Graal,* 4,018 ll. by ROBERT DE BORRON (BURUN), incomplete. End of XII.—(1) Francisque Michel, 1841 ; (2) De Douhet, 1855 (reprint of (1) in *Dict. des légendes du christianisme . . . publié par . . . Migne*).—*365.*—Robert probably belonged to Hertfordshire (*Z. f. rom. Ph.* xvi. 272, xxiii. 142). Others localize Robert's poem in France; its dialect is rather difficult to determine (Ziegler, *Über Sprache u. Alter des von R. de B. verf. Rom. du S. G.,* 1875 ; Sommer, *Messire R. de B. u. der Verf. des Didot-Perc.* 1908), and Robert's authorship itself is called in question. For editions of prose versions, see bibliography in Sommer, op. cit.; Wechssler, *Die Sage vom heil. G.* (1878), *Z.f.fr. S. u. L.* xxxvi. II. 7–71 (1910 Brugger); Jessie L. Weston, *The Quest of the Holy Grail*, 1913. 'Borron's work was probably composed in the closing years of the twelfth century, and it certainly formed the starting-point and model for the development of the combined Grail and Arthur themes as a formidable body of cyclic romance' (Miss Weston, p. 17). It is uncertain whether some of the numerous prose texts of *Saint Graal* were executed in England. Walter Map probably wrote on this theme, but no such work by him has come down to us.

37. *Roman d'Alexandre*, or *de toute chevalerie*, more than 12,000 ll., in laisses, by EUSTACHE or THOMAS DE KENT. End of XII.—Extr. in P. Meyer, *Alexandre le Grand*, i. 115 (1,550 ll.), ii. 278.—*212* (fragm. of 32 ll.), *293, 312, 367*.—Schneegans, *Z.f.fr. S. u. L.* xxx. 240, xxxi. 1, *Festschr. zum 12. d. Philologentage*, 1; Bauer, *Die Sprache des Fuerre de Gadres*, 1901 (also Schneegans in *Neuere Spr., Ergänzungsb.*, 1910); Weynand, *Der Roman de toute chev.*, 1911. P. Meyer places this romance in the early years of Henry III's reign, Schneegans in the second half of the XIIth century. This poem is the chief source of the Engl. *Kyng Alisaunder* (see a dissertation by Hildenbrand, Bonn, 1911). The principal source of Thomas's poem is Julius Valerius's *Epitome* (Weynand). An edition is being prepared by Schneegans.

38. *Waldef*, nearly 22,000 ll. End of XII.—*308* (cf. *Ro.* xii. 435).—Sachs, *Beitr. zur Kunde altfr., engl. u. prov. Liter.* (1837), 50 (dates the ms. as the XIIIth century). Cf. the Latin version, ed. R. Imelmann, *Johannes Bramis' Historia Regis Waldei* (Bonn, 1912).

§ 2. LAIS AND FABLIAUX

On the Lais see Ahlström, *Studier* (Bibliography). Breton lais in England are mentioned in *Roman de Renard*, ed. Martin, i. 67. On Fabliaux, see Bédier (Bibliography).

39. *Haveloc*, lai of 1,106 ll. *c.* 1130–40.—(1) Thomas Wright in *Metrical Chron. of Geffrey Gaimar* (1850); (2) Hardy and Martin in *Estorie des Engleis by Gaimar* (*Chron. and Memor.*, 1888).—*123, 303*.—Kupferschmidt in *Rom. Stud.* iv. 411; Heyman, *Studies on the Havelok-Tale* (Upsala, 1903); Deutschbein, *Studien*; Herbert Le Sourd Creek in *Engl. Stud.* xlviii. *Haveloc* has few A.-N. traits; it is based on Celto-Norse traditions. A shorter redaction is incorporated in Gaimar's *Chronicle*.

40. *Lai du cor*, 594 ll. by ROBERT BIKET. Middle of XII.—(1) Fr. Michel in Wolf, *Über die Lais*, 1841; (2) Wulff, 1888; (3) Dorner, 1907 (cf. *Jahresb. rom. Ph.* XI. i. 251; ii. 77).—*151*.—Few A.-N. traits; v. Richter in *Ausg. u. Abh.* xxxviii (1885). Based on Celtic traditions. This and *Haveloc* are the oldest lais, older than those of Marie de France.

41. *Lai del desirré*, 764 ll. 2nd half of XII.—Francisque Michel, *Lais inédits* (1836).—*303, 371*.

42. *Les trois savoirs*, fabliau of about 220 ll. End of XII.—Extr. in *Ro.* xxxvii. 219. Is wanting in *Recueil général des Fabliaux* and in Bédier's monograph; see also no. 53.—*309*.

43. *Le chevalier à la corbeille*, 264 ll. End of XII.—Montaiglon and Raynaud in *Recueil général*, ii. 183.—*78*.

§ 3. DIDACTIC LITERATURE. PROVERBS. ALLEGORY

44-6. *Disticha Catonis* (a popular collection of proverbs or aphorisms dating probably from the end of the third century) in three versions, ed. by Stengel in *Ausg. u. Abh.* xlvii (1886).

44. 766 ll. partly in stanzas of six ll. by ELIE DE WINCHESTER. *c.* 1140.—*82* (end of XII. according to *Biog. Brit. Lit.*, A.-N. Period, p. 125 (early XIIIth century according to ed.).—*198, 255*. On the versification, see ch. vii, p. 82.

45. 191 six-line stanzas by EVERART. End of XII.—Also Furnivall, *Minor Poems of the Vernon MS.* (E.E.T.S., 1901).— *97, 111, 131* (cf. *Inc.* 50), *184, 370*. On the versification see ch. vii, p. 82.

46. 1,078 ll. partly in six-line stanzas. End of XII.—*84*.

47-50. Four collections of *Proverbs* differing in parts from each other and from continental collections. End of XII.

47. *Li respit del curteis et del vilain*, 48 six-line stanzas with a concluding proverb.—Stengel in *Z. f. fr. S. u. L.* xiv. 154.—*182*.

48. *Proverbia magistri Serlonis*, 31 proverbs ; and

49. *Diversa proverbia*, 23 in number.—P. Meyer in *Docum. manuscr.*, 170.—*150*.—On the Latin original of Serlo, see ed., p. 139.

50. 363 *Proverbs.*—Stengel in *Z. f. fr. S. u. L.* xxi. 1 (cf. Tobler, *Proverbes au vilain*, 1895).—*177*.

51. *De Conjuge non ducenda*, 178 ll. by GAUVEIN. 2nd half of XII.— Thomas Wright in *Latin Poems . . . attributed to Walter Mapes* (Camden Soc., 1841).—*78, 163* (cf. *Bull. Soc. a. t.*, 1880, 77).

52. *On the choice of a husband*, five ten-line stanzas.—2nd half of XII.—P. Meyer, *Ro.* xiii. 512.—*307*.—The only A.-N. trait is the irregularity of the versification.

53. *Donnei des amants*, 1,244 ll. *c.* 1180.—G. Paris, *Ro.* xxv. 497.— *303*.—Contains counsels, examples, love-stories, and the fabliau *Les trois savoirs* (no. 42).

54. *Disciplina clericalis*, metrical translation in 3,700 ll. of the Latin original. End of XII.—(1) Barbazan, 1760; (2) Méon, 1808 (*Not. et Extr.* XXXIV. i. 209; see also Stengel, *Cod. Digby 86*, 11) ; (3) Hilka and Söderhjelm (Helsingfors, 1922).—*64, 82, 151, 304, 363, 397*. There is a sort of continuation of this poem in ms. *377*. It begins 'Empris ai cest ovre a fere', and may be entitled 'The man with two sweethearts'. Cf. *Bull. Soc. a. t.* (1887), 84, 91. Another translation, not A.-N., of the *Disc. cler.*, ibid. 83. Latin Original, ed. Hilka and Söderhjelm, 1912.

55. *Roman de Philosophie*, 1,658 ll. by SIMUND DE FREINE. End of XII. Matzke (*Soc. a. t.*, 1909).—*25, 163, 307*.

56. *Petit Plet*, 1,780 ll. by CHARDRY. End of XII.—Koch ; see nos. 20, 21.—Mss. same as nos. 20, 21 ; add *408*.—A debate between an old man and a youth on moral and social questions. The principal source is *Disticha Catonis*.

57. *On the human body*, allegory of 2,400 ll.—End of XII.—Extr. by P. Meyer in *Bull. Soc. a. t.* (1880), 49.—*163*.

§ 4. Satirical and Humorous Pieces

58. *Satire on the clergy,* 25 six-line stanzas (fragm.).—2nd half of XII.—P. Meyer in *Ro.* iv. 388.—*260.*

59. *Ragemon le bon,* 50 four-line stanzas. *c.* 1200.—Wright in *Anecdota litter.* (1844) 76.—*151.*—Stengel, *Cod. Digby 86,* 67. *Ragemon* or *Ragman* (see *Oxford Engl. Dict.*) is the Devil, and the ' Good Devil' is a kind of *bestourné* or *fatrasie*; cf. no. 266.

60. *Le blasme des fames* ('Quy femme prent a compagnie '), 190 ll. *c.* 1200.—(1) Wright, *Rel. Ant.* ii. 221 ; (2) Jubinal, *Nouv. Recueil,* ii. 330 (96 ll.) ; (3) P. Heyse, *Roman. Inedita,* 63.—*78* (Wright's and Jubinal's ed.), *406* (Heyse's ed.).—Other redactions, not A.-N., are indicated by P. Meyer, *Ro.* vi. 499; xv. 339 ; *Bull. Soc. a. t.* (1875) 27, 34 ; (1883) 77.

§ 5. Chronicles

See T. Duffus Hardy, *Descriptive Catalogue of Materials relating to the History of Great Britain and Ireland,* iii.

61. *Estorie des Engleis,* 6,532 ll. by Geffrey Gaimar. *c.* 1150.— (1) T. Wright, 1850; (2) T. Duffus Hardy and Trice-Martin (Rolls, 1888). —*12, 85* (fragm. by Imelmann in *Layamon, Versuch üb. seine Quellen,* 1906), *123, 311, 313.*—Vising, *Étude sur le dial. a.-n.* 1882 ; Gross, *Geffrei Gaimar, Die Kompos. &c.* 1902 (*Jahresber. rom. Ph.* VIII. ii. 9) ; Bell in *Mod. Lang. Rev.* xv. 170 (on the Prologue). Gaimar's source is, after he has reproduced the lay of *Haveloc,* the *Saxon Chronicle* (Gross). The first part of the Chronicle is wanting. This first part must have been closely related to the *Brut of Munich,* ed. Hofmann and Vollmöller (1877) from a ms. Codex Gallicus 7 in the Royal Library of Munich, ms. *414.* This poem contains 4,178 ll.— Cf. *Jahresber. rom. Ph.* X. ii. 110. Gaimar gives some details about himself (ll. 6436 ff.) ; he wrote his Chronicle for a 'dame Custance', probably the wife of a Yorkshire baron.

62. *Chronicle* of the war between the English and the Scots in 1173 and 1174, 2,071 ll. in 211 laisses by Jordan Fantosme. *c.* 1175.— Francisque Michel (Surtees Soc. 1840; also in *Chronique des Ducs de Normandie,* iii, 1844) ; Howlett (in *Chron. and Memor.* 1886).—*12, 313.*— Vising, *Étude sur le dial. a.-n.*; Rose in *Rom. Stud.* v. 301 (Fantosme's versification) ; Vising, *Sur la Versification a.-n.* (Upsala, 1884, 24). Jordan Fantosme was 'Magister' at Westminster, a pupil of Bishop Gilbert of Poitiers (ed. Howlett, p. lxii). His language has certain Poitevin traits. He probably lived some time in Norfolk (cf. ll. 896, 903, 1145, 1155, 1774, 1810) and was an eyewitness of what he relates.

63. *History of Peterborough,* about 600 ll. End of XII.—Sparke in *Historiæ Anglic. script. varii* (London, 1723), 241 ; a very bad text. The ms. was, according to ed., in the Cottonian collection, but is not to be found now.

§ 6. Natural Science.

64. *Computus,* 3,550 ll. by Philipe de Thaun. 1113 or 1119.— (1) T. Wright, as *Livre des Creatures* in *Popular Treatises on Science*

(1841), 20 ff. ; (2) Mall, 1873.—*36, 94, 101, 239, 314.*—P. Meyer in *Ro.* xl. 70; Fenge, *Sprachl. Untersuch. der Reime des C. (Ausg. u. Abh.* lv, 1886). An exposition of the calendar for the use of the clergy. Philipe indicates himself his sources : S. Augustine, Helperic, Bede, Gerland, Macrobius, Nebrot, Turkil (v. ll. 2080, 2360 ff.) and others ; but P. Meyer considers his work to be original. Cf. Haskins in *Rom. Rev.* v. 203. Of little or no value as literature, it is a precious linguistic document, being the oldest A.-N. work extant. Ch.-V. Langlois, *La connaissance de la nature et du monde au moyen âge*, 1911, pp. 1-48.

65. *Bestiarius (Bestiary)*, 2,890 ll. by PHILIPE DE THAUN. Between 112ᴵ and 1135.—(1) Wright (as in no. 64) ; (2) Walberg (Lund and Paris, 1900).—*36, 206, 417* (very much altered ; fragmentary). (N.B.—Lines 2891–3194 of the ed. belong to no. 67 ; see *Ro.* xxxviii. 482.) A translation of the Latin *Physiologus* (Walberg, p. xxvi).

66. *Lapidarius*, 1,710 ll. of six syllables, by PHILIPE DE THAUN. 1st half of XII.—P. Meyer, *Ro.* xxxviii. 496.— *261.*—Alphabetical order of the stones according to the Latin original (MS. B. Mus., Arundel 342 ; cf. P. Meyer, op. cit., 487).

67. *Lapidarius* in 304 octosyllabic ll. (fragm.) by PHILIPE DE THAUN. 1st half of XII.—Wright and Walberg in no. 65 (ll. 2891–3194).—*36.*—Philipe says in no. 66, l. 1709 : 'Ci fine li livre terrestre, E comence li celestre.' It is probable that the latter is our poem.

68. *Lapidarius* in prose. End of XII.—(1) P. Meyer, *Ro.* xxxviii. 271 ; (2) Mann (fragm. in *Rom. Forsch.* ii. 363).—*9, 383.* The sources are the Lapidarius 'Evax fut un mult riche reis' and the Latin Lapidarius of Marbod. A version (incomplete) of the XIIIth cent. is in ms. *272.* Cf. *M. L. R.* xvi. 37 (ms. *327 a*).

69. *Description of England*, 283 ll. 2nd half of XII.—Hardy and Trice-Martin in *Estorie des Engleis*, i. 278 (no. 61).—*311, 313.*—Conclusion : ' Descrist vus avum les cuntez Del païs e les eveskez E des chemins les quatre nons Or atant le vus lerrums.' Cf. ms. Cambridge C.C.C. 175.

70. *Letter of Prester John*, translation in 1,202 ll. by ROAU D'ARUNDEL. *c.* 1192.—Hilka in *Z. f. fr. S. u. L.* xliii. 100.—*304.*—A translation, with some additions, of a Latin original (see ed., p. 84). Cf. P. Meyer in *Not. et Extr.* xxxiv. i. 228.

§ 7. LEGAL WORKS.

Anglo-Norman began to be used in legal documents in the XIIth century, but the law texts ascribable to this century have come down much altered in mss. of later date, and will therefore be included in the following chapter, B, § 11 (see nos. 331, 332).

III.   THE THIRTEENTH CENTURY
A.   Religious Literature
§ 1.   THE BIBLE

71. *Miroir* or *Evangiles des domees*, more than 20,000 ll. by ROBERT DE GRETHAM. 1st half of XIII.—Extr. in *Z. f. rom. Ph.* i. 543 (Varnhagen).—*Ro.* xv. 298, xxxii. 29 (P. Meyer).—*112, 226, 276, 320, 333* (two mss.; see *Ro.* xlii. 145), *379* (mostly incomplete).—This poem, a sort of theological encyclopaedia, is an exposition of the gospels of the Sundays (*domées*). Among the sources are S. Gregory and S. Fursius; cf. *Ro.* xv. 296. The poem is dedicated to dame Aline, evidently the wife of Alain (cf. 249).

72. *Commentary on the Proverbs of Solomon,* in prose. Early XIII.—(1) Extr. in *Not. et Extr.* XXXV. i. 136; (2) Le Compte, *The Sources of the Anglo-French Commentary on the Prov. of S.* (Collegeville, 1906).—*369.*—Principal source: Petrus Comestor, or Petrus of Rheims. P. Meyer's supposition that this Commentary was an original work is to be rejected. It is doubtful whether this work is A.-N. or continental. The present writer favoured the second alternative in an article in *Jahresb. rom. Ph.* x. ii. 110, but, considering that all the works copied by the first four hands of the ms. containing this work were composed in England, is inclined to regard this work also as A.-N. Cf. *Not. et Extr.* XXXV. i. 131.

73, 74. *The Passion of Christ,* two metrical versions of the 1st half of the XIIIth cent.

73. About 1,000 ll. Extr. in *Ro.* xxxii. 38 (P. Meyer).—*276.*

74. *Chansun de la Passiun,* 75 ll. in irregular stanzas.—Reinsch in *Arch. n. Spr.* lxiii. 95.—*134.*—N.B.—The Passion printed by Foster in *The Northern Passion* (E.E.T.S.) is probably of continental origin, though it exists in several A.-N. mss. Cf. *Hist. litt.* xxxiii. 355, and *Ro.* xxxii. 102.

75. *La Genesi N. D. Seinte Marie,* 3,410 ll. 1st half of XIII.— (1) Extr. in Francisque Michel, *Rapports,* p. 255; (2) Becker, *Das La Genesi N. D. S. M. betitelte Gedicht* (Greifswald, 1908). An edition by Prof. Tanquerey (cf. *L'Évol.,* p. xv, n. 2.) is in preparation.—*51* (the poem that follows in the ms. is by Herman de Valenciennes, not an A.-N. poem, as Tanquerey supposes, *L'Évol.,* p. xiv).—This poem is a paraphrase of the *Passion of Christ and Mary,* with a prologue, summarizing the Old Testament. The principal source is, of course, the Bible; for other sources, see Becker.—N.B. The *Genealogy of Mary,* 72 ll. in mss. *42, 211,* is probably continental.

76-8. Three translations of the Apocalypse, with Commentary.

76. The Trinity College Apocalypse, in prose. *c.* 1240, partly published by Montague Rhodes James (Roxburghe Club, 1909). Cf. Berger, *La Bible,* p. 93.—*299* (probably executed at St. Albans).—The text is closely related to that of the ms. *350* (B. N., f. fr. 1768; cf. Berger, p. 93), and the commentary to the Latin Commentary published by Coxe (Roxburghe Club, 1876; ibid. p. 97). Several other A.-N. mss. contain the *Apocalypse,* e. g. *13, 17* ('one of the finest mss. extant', Berger, p. 85).

77. Metrical translation of nearly 4,600 ll., by WILLIAM GIFFARD. 2nd half of XIII.—Extr. by Fox in *Mod. Lang. Notes,* viii.—*419.*

78. Metrical translation, in 1,431 ll. 2nd half of XIII. P. Meyer in *Ro.* xxv. 187.—Mss. (differing very much) *2, 110, 243, 271, 302* (formerly MacLean), *398, 418.*—Cf. *Ro.* xv. 330; xxiv. 361; xxv. 174

(P. Meyer). The Commentary adjoined to the poem is not originally A.-N.

79-81. The Childhood of Christ was treated in three poems of the XIIIth century on the basis of the *Evangelium Nicodemi*.

79. 2,115 ll. of the end of the century.—G. Paris and A. Bos in *Trois Versions rimées de l'Évangile de Nicodème* (Soc. a. t.).—*134* (according to P. Meyer, *Ro.* x. 622, of the first half of XIV., according to ed., p. xlvi, of the end of XIII.). A full bibliography is given by Gast in *Die beiden Redactionen des Évangile de l'Enfance* (Greifswald, 1909), pp. vii, xxvii.—N.B. Chrestien's poem on the same subject is hardly A.-N. in spite of P. Meyer's assertion in *Bull. Soc. a. t.*, 1898, p. 81 and *Hist. litt.* xxxiii. 356. Cf. ed. of Paris and Bos, p. xiii.

80. 504 four-line stanzas.—Gast, in the work cited above.—*181, 226* (fragm.). This poem is a *remaniement* of a continental version, in which the *remanieur* has attempted to turn the original rhymes into stanzas. The difficulties encountered are visible in the rhymes and *enjambements* of the new text (cf. *Jahresb. rom. Ph.* XII. ii. 139). On the versification, see below, ch. vii. A ms. of Grenoble and a ms. Didot, noticed by P. Meyer, *Hist. litt.* xxxiii. 356, give a continental version; cf. also Gast.

81. 121 ll.—*246.*—Cf. P. Meyer, *Hist. litt.* xxxiii. 356.

82. Prose version of the *Childhood of Christ*, followed by lives of four of the Apostles.—*78.*—Ward, *Catal.* i. 328.

83. *The last hours of Christ*, 75 ll. XIII.—Reinsch in *Arch. n. Spr.* lxiii. 54.—*134.*—N.B. *La Passioun Notre Seignour* (ms. Harley, 2253) in the bibliography of Tanquerey (*L'Évol.*, p. xvii) is a poem by Herman de Valenciennes.

84-6. *Annunciation of Mary*, in three metrical versions.

84. Ten three-line stanzas (with Latin refrain).—P. Meyer, *Ro.* iv. 372.—*15.*

85. Five eleven-line stanzas.—P. Meyer, *Bull. Soc. a. t.*, 1893, 40.—*7.*

86. Six-line stanzas by NICHOLAS BOZON. End of XIII.—Extr. by P. Meyer in *Ro.* xiii. 519.—*152* (cf. *Inc.* 198), *307.*

87-93. *Joys of Mary*, seven poems of the XIIIth century, most of them in prayer form.

87. 14 stanzas of six (or more) lines.—T. Wright in *Specimens of Lyric Poetry* (1842), 54.—*78.*

88. 25 four-line stanzas.—Extr. by P. Meyer, *Ro.* xxxv. 574; Stengel, *Cod. Digby 86*, 81.—*134, 142, 151* (only five stanzas), *255, 307* (cf. *Inc.*, p. 36).

89. 70 ll.—P. Meyer, *Ro.* xv. 307.—*226.*

90. 65 ll.—P. Meyer, *Ro.* xxxv. 571, q. v. for mss., and *Inc.* 148.—*60, 134, 142, 288.*

91, 92. Two short poems, ed. Reinsch, in *Arch. n. Spr.* lxiii. 56, 93, from ms. Lambeth 522 (no. *134*).

93. 15½ twelve-line stanzas, probably by MARTIN, a friar of Bury St. Edmunds.—Priebsch, *M. L. R.* iv. 73.—*6.*

94. *The Five Joys of Mary* in prose.—Extr. by Stengel, *Cod. Digby 86*, 6.—*151.*—These *Five Joys* are often to be found in prayer-books

or primers; cf. Priebsch, *M. L. R.* iv. 71; *Arch. n. Spr.* lxiii. 66, 75;
Bull. Soc. a. t. (1881) 47, (1901) 79.

95, 96. *Lament of Mary*, two poems.

95. 675 ll. of 16 syllables, according to P. Meyer in *Ro.* xv. 309;
1,240 ll. of 8 and 7 syllables, according to Professor Tanquerey.—Late
XIII.—F. J. Tanquerey, 1921.—*169* (fragm.), *226.*

96. 42 four-line stanzas by NICHOLAS BOZON. Late XIII. or early
XIV.—(1) T. Wright in the *Chronicle of Pierre de Langtoft*, ii. 438 (see
no. 377); (2) Tanquerey together with no. 95.—*4, 29, 307.*

§ 2. SAINTS' LIVES

97. See P. Meyer in *Hist. litt. de la France*, xxxiii. *60 Miracles
of Mary* (and some other saints). Early XIII.—Extr. by (1) Wolter
in *Der Judenknabe* (Bibl. Norm. ii.), 115; (2) Neuhaus, *Adgar's
Marienlegenden*, 2, 28; (3) Mussafia, *Stud. zu d. mittelalt. Marienleg.* iv. 34, 53; Kjellman, *Une Version anglo-n. inédite du Miracle
de S. Théophile* and *Le Miracle de la femme enceinte* in *Stud. i
Mod. Språkvetenskap* (Upsala, 1914); ed. Kjellman, 1922.—*25, 226*
(only one item: Friar suffering from cancer; extr. *Ro.* xv. 328).—
Ward, *Catal.* ii. 728; P. Meyer in *Not. et Extr.* XXXIV. ii. 33. These
Miracles much resemble, in content and form, the *Miracles* of Adgar
(no. 13), and are from the same source.

98. *Three Miracles of Mary*, about 1,000 ll. by EVERARD DE
GATELEY. 2nd half of XIII.—Extr. by (1) Stengel in *Z. f. fr. S. u. L.*
xiv. 129; (2) P. Meyer, *Ro.* xv. 272, xxix. 36.—*180, 222* (fragment).—
Everard was a friar of St. Edmundsbury (Suffolk), and drew from a
Latin original (*Ro.* xxix. 30).

99. *The Harper of Rochester*, miracle of Mary in 95 ll. 1st half of
XIII.—Francisque Michel in *Eustache le Moine* (1834), 108.—*54.*

100. *Vie de S. Laurent*, 950 ll. Early XIII. Söderhjelm, Paris,
1888.—*121, 364.*—For the Latin original see *Acta Sanctorum*, Aug.
ii. 489 (cf. ed., p. xxxii).

101. *Thomas of Canterbury*, 422 ll. (fragm. of a poem of about
8,000 ll.). *c.* 1220.—P. Meyer, *Fragments d'une Vie de S. Th.* (Soc. a. t.,
1885).—*395.*—The source is the *Quadrilogus.*

102-6. *Patrick's Purgatory*, in five metrical redactions, all based on a
Latin treatise, for which see Mall, *Rom. Forsch.* vi. 139 seq., Ward,
Catal. ii. 445, Mörner, *Le Purgatoire...f. fr. 25545* (Lund, 1920), p. vii.

102. 1,762 ll. Early XIII (or older).—Extr. by Kölbing in *Engl.
Stud.* i. 61 (frz.[2]); Ward, *Catal.* ii. 468.—*49.*

103. 221 four-line stanzas by BÉROUL. Early XIII.—Marianne
Mörner (Lund, 1917).—*304* (incomplete), *401.*—*Not. et Extr. des mss.*
XXXIV. i. 241.

104. 858 ll. Early XIII.—Vising (Göteborg, 1916).—*60, 352.*—Kölbing in *Engl. Stud.* i. 60 (frz.[3]); Ward, *Catal.* ii. 471.

105. 1,790 ll. 1st half of XIII.—Extr. by P. Meyer in *Ro.* vi. 154.—
220.—According to Miss Mörner (ed. of no. 103, p. xix) same text as
the following.

106. Fragment of about 120 ll., of which 40 are mutilated. 1st half
of XIII (or older).—Extr. by Kölbing in *Eng. Stud.* i. 71 (frz.[4]);
Ward, *Catal.* ii. 474.—*89.*

107. *Modwenna*, about 8,000 ll. Early XIII.—Extr. in Suchier, *Über die Vie de S. Auban* (1876), 54.—*149, 330.*—The original is a *Vita* by Geoffrey, Abbot of Burton (Suchier).

108. *Life of S. Gregory*, 2,954 ll., and *Gregory's Dialogues*, nearly 24,000 ll., by ANGIER. The *Dialogues* were written in 1212, the *Life* in 1214.—Ed. of the *Life* by P. Meyer in *Ro.* xii. 152; extr. from the *Dialogues* in Cloran, *The Dialogues of Gregory the Great translated into Anglo-Norman French by Angier* (Strassburg, 1901).—*368*, probably autograph.—Miss Mildred K. Pope, *Étude sur la langue de frère Angier* (Oxford and Paris, 1904); Cloran, op. cit.—Angier was a friar of St. Frideswide's, near Oxford. His original for the Life of St. Gregory is a *Vita* by Johannes Diaconus (IXth cent.). The *Dialogues* are mostly tales about Italian monks.

109. *John the Patriarch*, 7,732 ll. Early XIII.—Extr. by P. Meyer, *Not. et Extr.* xxxviii. 296.—*294.*

110. *Pope Clement*, about 15,000 ll. (incomplete). Early XIII.— Extr. P. Meyer, op. cit., 312.—*294.*—On the versification see ch. vii.

111-14. Four pieces by HENRY D'ARCI. 1st half of XIII.

111. *Verba Seniorum* or *Vitas Patrum*, about 4,200 ll.—Extr. in *Not. et Extr.* xxxv. 140, 161.—*78, 369.*—The Latin original, *Verba Seniorum*, for which see *Not. et Extr.*, loc. cit., 138, and *Hist. litt.* xxxiii. 254, is a collection of *memorabilia* of the hermits of the Thebaid and episodes in their lives.

112. *Thaïs*, 168 ll.—P. Meyer in *Not. et Extr.*, loc. cit. Same mss. and source as 111.

113. *Antichrist*, 342 ll.—Kastner, *M. L. R.* i. 271.—*4, 369.*

114. *S. Paul's descent to Hell*, 273 ll.—Extr. in *Not. et Extr.* xxxv. i. 156.—*369.*—Henry d'Arci wrote his poems at Temple Bruer, Lincolnshire, apparently in the 1st half of the XIIIth cent. P. Meyer places him at the beginning of the cent. (*Not. et Extr.* 139 ff.), in the 2nd half in *Hist. litt.* xxxiii. 258. Kastner (270) thinks that he wrote his *Antichrist* about the middle of the cent.

115. *Alban*, 1,845 ll. in 48 laisses. 1st half of XIII.—Atkinson, *Vie de S. Auban*, 1876.—*341.*—Suchier, *Über die M. Paris zugeschriebene Vie d. S. A.*, 1876; Uhlemann in *Rom. Stud.* iv (1880).—The probable original is a Latin text, which goes back to Bede. Even the rubrics of the poem are rhymed and make a total of 464 ll. They are probably not by the author of the life (Uhlemann, 557).

116. *Seth*, about 300 ll. Mid-XIII.—*246* (not *245* as in *Hist. litt.* xxxiii. 375).

117-21. *Margaret*, in five metrical versions, of which the first-named seems to belong to the beginning of the XIIIth cent.

117. 85 four-line stanzas. Extr. in Herbert, *Ro.* xxxii. 396.—*116.*

118. 68 laisses, usually of six lines.—*319.*

119. 478 ll.--(1) Scheler in *Deux rédactions diverses de la lég. de S. M.* (Antwerp, 1877); (2) Joly (Paris, 1879).—*364.*

120. 614 ll. Ed. P. Meyer, *Ro.* xl. 540.—*102.*

121. 330 ll. by BOZON. *c.* 1300.—*51.* N.B.—A fragment published by Zingerle, *Rom. Forsch.* vi. 414, seems to be continental.

122. *Richard of Chichester*, 1,696 ll. by PIERRE DE PECKAM or

D'ABERNUN. 1267-8.—Baker in *Rev. d. langues rom.* liii.—*330* (probably autograph). On the Latin original see Ed., p. 247.

123. *S. Edmund de Pontigny*, Archbishop of Canterbury, 2,018 ll. 2nd half of XIII.—Extr. in *Rev. d. langues rom.* liv. 215.—*330.*—Cf. *Hist. litt.* xxxiii. 346.

124. *Mary of Egypt*, 406 ll. 2nd half of XIII.—*25.* (Cf. *Inc.* 252.)

125-7. *Edward the Confessor* in three metrical versions.

125. 4,680 ll. 1245.—Luard (Rolls, 1858).—*218.*—Fritz,*Über Verfasser u. Quellen der altfr. Estoire d. S. Aedw.* (Heidelberg, 1910). The author was probably a monk at Westminster.—The principal source is *Vita S. Edwardi Regis* by Alred de Rieval.

126. 5,227 ll.—Extr. in Ed. Luard, p. 384.—*407.*

127. 4,225 ll.—Extr. in *M. L. R.* iii. 374, and *Rev. d. langues rom.* liv. 213 (Baker).—*330.* Private fragment. A prose version exists of this poem : see *Hist. litt.* xxxiii. 347 ; *Ro.* xl. 45.

128-30. *Eustache* or *Placidas* in three metrical versions.

128. 896 ll. by GUILLAUME DE FERRIÈRES; A.-N. according to P. Meyer, *Hist. litt.* xxxiii. 348 (1906) ; another opinion, idem, *Not. et Extr.* XXXIV. i. 225 (1891).—*319.*—Suchier, *Gesch. d. franz. Lit.* 186.

129. 1,250 ll.—*340.*

130. Fragment of 12 mutilated six-line stanzas.—Stengel, *Cod. Digby 86*, 126.—*199.*—*Not. et Extr.* XXXIV. i. 225-8. On Latin sources of this legend see Ott in *Rom. Forsch.* xxxii. 483.—The poem of ms. *119* (*Not. et Extr.* l. c.) is not A.-N.

131. *Francis*, 9,272 ll.—*360.*

132. *Antichrist*, about 2,000 ll.—Extr. in *Ro.* xxix. 79.—*180.*—Stengel in *Z. f. fr. S. u. L.* xiv. 137, where the poem is described as a treatise on the end of the world, which is a favourite theme of the author.

133. *S. Paul's descent to Hell*, fragm. of 282 ll. *c.* 1300.—P. Meyer, *Ro.* xxiv. 365 (589).—*243, 398.*

134. *11 Metrical Legends of saints*, probably by NICHOLAS BOZON, *c.* 1300. Two are of male saints : *Paphnuce*, 214 ll. ; *Paul the Hermit*, 914 ll., both published by Baker, *Ro.* xxxviii. 420, and *M. L. R.* iv. 494, from ms. *330.* The Latin sources are for *Paphnuce* principally the *Historia Lusiaca*, for *S. Paul*, Jerome and the *Legenda aurea.* Nine are of female saints : *Agatha* 208 ll., *Agnes* 303 ll., *Christina* 164 ll., *Elisabeth of Hungary* 414 ll., *Juliana* 175 ll., *Lucy* 177 ll., *Margaret* 330 ll., *Martha* 340 ll., *Mary Magdalen* 504 ll.—all in ms. *51*, *Elisabeth* also in ms. *330*, which alone has been published in full, by Karl in *Z. f. rom. Ph.* xxxiv. 305; of *Agnes* there are extracts in *Contes moralisés de Nicole Bozon* by P. Meyer, p. xlviii.

135-6. *Mary Magdalen* in two metrical versions.

135. Fragm. of 42 ll. in five-line stanzas. End of XIII.—*319.*—*Hist. litt.* xxxiii. 368.

136. Fragm. of 13 six-line stanzas.—(1) Suchier in *Z. f. rom. Ph.* iv. 362 ; (2) Doncieux in *Ro.* xxii. 266.—*415.*

137. *Osith*, 1,694 ll.—Baker in *M. L. R.* vi. 483.—*330.*—The greater part of the poem belongs to the end of the XIIth century and the rest to the XIIIth century. It is difficult to indicate a precise original. Cf. *Jahresb. rom. Ph.* XIII. ii. 85.

138. *Faith*, 1,241 ll. by SIMON DE WALSINGHAM.—Extr. in *Rev. d. langues rom.* liv. 219.—*330*.

139. *Judas*, about 300 ll.—Extr. in P. Meyer, *Docum. manuscr.* 242.—*173*.

140. *Vision of Tundal*, fragm. of 364 ll. in laisses.—Friedel and Meyer in *La Vision de Tondale* (Paris, 1907), 67.—*339* (cf. *M. L. R.* xiii. 313).— On the Latin original, see Ed.—Cf. Schofield, *Engl. Liter.* 399.

§ 3. SERMONS AND RELIGIOUS TREATISES

141-4. Prose sermons.

141. Short prose sermons in ms. *275*.

142. Fifty-five short prose sermons in ms. *284*.

143. Several sermons, mostly in prose, in ms. *282*.—Extr. in *Ro.* xxxii. 106; cf. *164*, *364*. These sermons have few A.-N. traits and may belong to the XIIth century.

144. Several prose sermons in mss. *188* (ff. 1-29, 37-46) and *200* (ff. 179-251).

145-52. Metrical sermons.

145. ' Homme quant est de femme nez ', about 600 ll.—Extr. in *Bull. Soc. a. t.* (1880) 55.—*163*.

146-7. ' Oyez, seignurs, sermun ', about 1,920 ll. in (mostly) six-line stanzas ; ed. Tanquerey (in no. 25). ' Ci commence un sermun petit ', beginning in verse and continuing in prose.—*25*.

148. ' Une petite parole, seignurs, escotez ', 126 ll. Middle of XIII.— T. Wright, *Specimens of Lyric Poetry*, 76.—*78*.

149. ' Par la priere de un men compagnon ', 52 ll. by SIMON DE KERNERTHIN (probably Caermarthen in Wales).—Stengel, *Z. f. fr. S. u. L.* xiv. 150.—*182*.

150-1. ' Ky ke faus sovent en diz ', 14 four-line stanzas ; ' Deu vus dura grant honur ', 16 four-line stanzas.—P. Meyer in *Ro.* xxxii. 37, 41.—*276*.

152. Seven short metrical sermons by NICHOLAS BOZON. *c.* 1300.— Extr. *Ro.* xiii. 522 (nos. 25-31).—*307*.—Cf. *Les Contes moralisés de N. Bozon*, p. xlv.

153. *Chasteau d'Amour*, 1,168 ll., an exposition of Christian doctrine by ROBERT GROSSETESTE. 1st half of XIII.—(1) Cooke in *Carmina Anglo-Normannica* (Caxton Soc. 1852) ; (2) J. Murray (Paris, 1918).— Numerous mss., among which are nos. *25*, *74*, *134*, *145*, *161*, *170*, *173*, *194*, *302*, *348*.—Cf. Murray, pp. 22-33.—On Grosseteste see *D. N. B.* Stevenson, *R. Gr.* (London, 1899), and Murray. An episode in this poem is the allegory of *God's four daughters* (cf. no. 289).—Principal sources : Hugo de S. Victor, S. Bernard, and the Gospel of Luce (see Murray). On English translations see Haase, *Anglia*, xii. 311 ; Hupe, ibid. xiv. 415.

154. *On the Love of God*, 780 ll. Mid-XIII (earlier according to Tanquerey, *L'Évol.*, p. xvii).—(1) P. Meyer, *Ro.* xxix. 9 (83) ; (2) Extr. in Francisque Michel, *Rapports*, p. 256.—*25*, *51*, *96*, *180*, *255*, *340*, *348* (cf. *Inc.*, pp. 58, 358). Some mss. begin ' Chekun deyt estre amé ', others ' Seint Pol li apostre dist '.—Among the sources is the *Vers de* *la Mort* by Helinand. Part of this poem is incorporated in the *Manuel des pechez* (no. 158).

155. *Dialogue between S. Julian and his disciple*, about 2,000 ll. Middle of XIII.—Extr. in *Ro*. xxix. 22.—*4, 180.*—The subject is sin and justice.

156. *Mireour de l'Église*, also called 'sermon', prose translation of *Speculum Ecclesie* by Edmond de Pontigny. Mid-XIII.—(1) Extr. in *Bull. Soc. a. t.* (1880) 72; (2) *Ro*. xxix. 53 (P. Meyer).—*7, 74, 163, 180, 182, 188, 279, 359* (cf. P. Meyer, op. cit., and Stengel, *Z. f. fr. S. u. L.* xiv. 135; *Hist. litt.* xviii. 253).

157. *Lumiere as lais*, about 15,000 ll. by PIERRE DE PECKHAM or D'ABERNUN. 1267-8.—Extr. in *Ro*. viii. 328; xv. 288 (P. Meyer).—*13, 16, 83,145, 226, 267, 321, 338, 378, 403.*—ms. *321* is probably autograph; cf. *Ro*. viii. 325; *Rev. d. l. rom.* liii. 246; *Inc.* 436.—A kind of theological encyclopaedia on the basis of the *Elucidarius* of Honorius of Autun.

158. *Manuel des pechez*, about 11,200 ll., theological encyclopaedia by WILHAM DE WADINGTON. End of XIII.—(1) Ed., incomplete, by Furnivall in Roberd of Brunne's *Handlyng Synne* (E.E.T.S. 1901, 1903); (2) Extr. in Jubinal, *Nouveau Rec.* ii. 304.—*60, 61* (fragm.), *84, 86, 170, 217, 226, 235, 267, 317, 319, 326, 331, 333* (fragm.), *362.* Cf. *Ro*. viii. 333, xxix. 47, xlii. 145; *Hist. litt.* xxviii. 179.—Wilham's sources are, among many others, the Bible, Gregory the Great, *Vitas Patrum*, &c.; see Gaston Paris in *Hist. litt.* xxviii. 193. Robert of Brunne's *Handlyng Synne* is a free verse translation. For an English translation in prose see Hope Emily Allen in *Mod. Phil.* xiii. 743.

159. *On Christian Love*, six eight-line stanzas. Mid-XIII.—Stengel, in *Cod. Digby 86*, 128.—*134, 151, 162.*—Reinsch, *Arch. n. Spr.* lxiii. 57; P. Meyer, *Ro*. xiii. 518.—A fragment of similar contents is indicated *Inc.* 335, as existing in MS. Cott. Cleop. C. v, which I have not seen, and which also may be A.-N.

160. *On the Love of Mary*, six-line stanzas—Extr. in *Ro*. xiii. 531.—*307.*

161-2. *Christ speaks to the human soul*, two poems.—Reinsch in *Arch. n. Spr.* lxiii. 61 (about 150 ll.) and p. 95 (75 ll.).—*134.*

163. *Christ speaks to the sinners*, 20 ll.—Extr. in *Ro*. xiii. 518.—*307.*

164. *On the death of Christ*, about 200 ll.—Extr. in Reinsch, *Arch. n. Spr.* lxiii. 76.—*134, 257.*

165. *On the Mortal Sins*, unrhymed ll. on each of the 7 sins.—J. C. Fox, *M. L. R.* viii. 350 (cf. *Ro*. xxxii. 40).—*258, 276.*

166. Prose treatises on Sin, Confession, the X Commandments, etc.—Extr. Stengel in *Cod. Digby 86*, pp. 1-3.—*134, 151.*

167. Similar treatises in Oxford mss., as *144* (ff. 1-77), *148, 172, 175, 197.*

168. *Exhortation to Confession*, several formularies and treatises in the following mss.: *134, 151, 197, 226, 280, 285, 364.*—*Arch. n. Spr.* lxiii. 64, 78; *Ro*. xv. 332, 340; xxxii. 95, 110.

169. *Robert Grosseteste's Confession*, prose.—Urtel in *Z. f. rom. Ph.* xxxiii. 573.—*412.*

170. *On Penitence*, two prose tracts in ms. *298*, one very extensive. —Cf. ms. *134*, fol. 596.

171. *On Penitence*, 45 five-line stanzas by SIMON DE KERNERTHIN. —Stengel in *Z. f. fr. S. u. L.* xiv. 147.—*182*.

172. *The X Commandments*, with short religious and moral tracts.— *270, 298*.

173. *Paraphrases of the Creed*; three small poems in mss. *142, 226, 228*; ed. P. Meyer, *Ro.* xxxv. 577; xv. 321 (in lines of 16 syllables), 341; in prose in ms. *284*.

174-5. *On Monachism*, two prose tracts.—*298, 307* (whereof extracts in *Ro.* xiii. 513). Cf. ms. Cambridge, John's Coll. E. I.

176. *On Trentel*, prose tract.—P. Meyer, *Ro.* xv. 282.—*224*.

177. *On Death*, 10 six-line and three-line stanzas, probably by NICHOLAS BOZON.—Reinsch in *Arch. n. Spr.* lxiii. 76.—*102, 134, 307.*—*Ro.* xiii. 526.

178-9. *On the Vanity of earthly Life*, two poems.

178. 234 ll.—Reinsch, *Arch. n. Spr.* lxiii. 59.—*134*.

179. 337 ll.—Extr. in *M. L. R.* xiii. 312.—*339*.

180. *Legend of the Holy Rood*, prose tract.—Extr. in *Ro.* xv. 326; xxxii. 74.—*167, 226, 279, 403*.—On the Latin source see *Ro.* xv. 326; xvi. 253.

181. *The name of Jesus*, 138 ll.—Reinsch, *Arch. n. Spr.* lxiii. 70.— *134*.

182. *La distinctioun de la estature Jhesu Crist*, prose tract.—*78*.

183. *The seven gifts of the Holy Ghost*, prose tract.—*60*.

§ 4. RELIGIOUS POETRY

184. *Prayers and Hymns.* A great many manuscripts contain larger or smaller collections of prayers and hymns, which have been only partly published. The date of these pieces, which are mostly metrical, is difficult to establish; a few may belong to the XIIth or to the XIVth century; but the majority are certainly of the XIIIth century. They are here cited by the numbers of our List of MSS.

6. Ward, *Catal.* ii. 128; *Inc.* 32.

14. Four prayers quoted *Inc.* 36, 37.

78. Prayer to Mary, 13 four-line stanzas.—T. Wright, *Spec. Lyric Poetry*, 65.—English and French prayer to Mary, beginning 'Mayden moder milde, Oyez cel oreyson', 68 ll. ibid. 97.

96. Ward, *Catal.* iii. 293, *Inc.* 32; Nætebus, *Strophenformen*, 71.

134. Reinsch in *Arch. n. Spr.* lxiii. 55-94.

151. Stengel, *Cod. Digby 86*, passim. Among the numerous prayers in this ms. there may be named especially *Litania Sanctorum*, 'Gloriouse reine, heiez de moi merci', 24 four-line stanzas. This poem exists also in *134, 142, 255, 307.* Cf. *Inc.* 149 and 36.

209. French and Latin prayers to Mary and other saints.

221. A prayer-book; cf. James, *Catal.* and *Ro.* xv. 270.

226. *Ro.* xv. 306, 322: prayers to Mary.

227. ibid., 341 ff.

265. A prayer-book. Cf. James's *Catal.*

307. Prayers, some by NICHOLAS BOZON. Cf. *Ro.* xiii. 508 ff.
339, 340. Neuphil. Mitteil. (1911), 12 ; *Ro.*xliv.132; *M.L.R.*xiii.312.
185. The Lord's prayer, paraphrased and glossed.—*142, 226, 227, 307, 384.*—The glosses of ms. *384* are published by P. Meyer in *Jahrb.f.r.e. L.* vii. 53 ; for the others see Långfors in *Neuphil. Mitteil.* (1912), 35, 43.
186. *Expositiun Adam de Eccestre sur la pater nostre,* in prose.—*273.*
187. *Hymn to God* in quatrains.—*141* (cf. *Inc.* 434).—Another hymn, ' Domedieu de grant empris ', in *90* is cited *Inc.* 76.
188-91. *Prayers, Aves, and Hymns to Christ* in the following editions or extracts.
188. Three four-line stanzas.—P. Meyer, *Ro.* iv. 371.—*63.*
189. Two prayers in lines of 16 syllables.—P. Meyer, *Ro.* xxxii. 110.—*285.*
190. 51 four-line stanzas. Extr. *Bull. Soc. a. t.* (1880) 74.—*6, 96, 163.*—Cf. *Inc.* p. 32.
191. 12 four-line stanzas, attributed to EDMOND DE PONTIGNY, in 5 mss., some of which have already been cited above. (Cf. *Neuphil. Mitteil.* (1911), 15.) Ed. Bentley (1831), Wallace (1893); see *Inc.,* p. 107.
192. French and English prayer in eight four-line stanzas.—P. Meyer, *Ro.* xxxii. 23.—*276.*
193. Metrical prayer cited *Ro.* xxxvi. 184.—*79.*
194-6. *Prayers to the Holy Ghost.*
194. Translation of ' Veni, sancte spiritus ', five six-line stanzas.—P. Meyer, *Ro.* xxxii. 26.—*276.*
195. Translation of ' Veni, creator spiritus ', 36 ll.—Extr. in Stengel, *Cod. Digby 86,* 10 (cf. *Ro.* xv. 272).—*151, 221.*
196. 12 six-line stanzas.—Stengel, *Z. f. fr. S. u. L.* xiv. 146.—*182.*
197-201. *Prayers and Aves to Mary.*
197. Metrical prayer ' Douce dame, jeo vous pri '.—*202* (apparently of XIIth century).
198. Metrical Salutations.—*60, 103, 118.*—*Inc.* 76, 77, 78, 97.
199. 38 four-line stanzas.—F. Wolf, *Über die Lais* (1841), 438.—*95.*
200. Six stanzas of unequal length, translated from a Latin original.—Ed. ibid., 475.—*95.*
201. French and Latin prayer, six eight-line stanzas.—T. Wright, *Rel. Ant.* i. 200.—*84.*
202. *Matins of Mary,* about 1,300 ll.—*60.*—*Inc.* 397.
203. *Paraphrase of the Hail Mary,* 16 four-line stanzas.—Extr. *Ro.* xv. 306.—*226.*—Nætebus, op. cit. 91.
204. *Prayer to S. Catherine,* nine eight-line stanzas.—Wright, *Rel. Ant.* i. 106; P. Meyer, *Rec. d'anc. textes,* 375.—*118.*
205. *Prayer to S. Francis,* five four-line stanzas.—P. Meyer, *Ro.* xv. 271.—*221.*
206. *Prayer to S. Nicholas,* six six-line stanzas.—P. Meyer, *Ro.* iv. 374.—*210.*
207. *Request to Winteney Abbey,* 24 ll. by FRÈRE SIMON.—P. Meyer, *Jahrb.f. r. e. L.* vii. 47.—*35* (autograph).

208. 'Jhesu Crist, par ta ducur', 56 ll.—Reinsch, *Arch. n. Spr.* lxiii. 77.—*134.*

209. 'Quaunt le russinol se cesse', 12 eight-line stanzas.—Petersen, *Neuphil. Mitteil.* (1911) 20.—*340.*—N.B. These two poems are prayers or laments.—A prose lament in *Arch. n. Spr.* lxiii. 92.—(*134*). The lament 'Jay un quer mut let', published by Stengel, *Cod. Digby 86*, 30, and often copied in England, is not A.-N. Cf. *Ro.* xli. 217.

210. 'Queor ke tut volt aver si ke ren ne li faille', religious poem of about 400 alexandrines.—*25.*—Ward, *Catal.* ii. 728.

211. Religious poems by NICHOLAS BOZON.—*307.*—*Ro.* xiii. 500 *et passim*; particularly a poem on the *Life to come*, begin. 'Ben e Mal unt fet covenant', ibid., p. 523, in a metrical form often used by Bozon : six-line stanzas, the third and sixth with lines shorter than the others.

B.   Secular Literature

§ 1.   ROMANCES

212. *Guy de Warwick*, 12,762 ll. (ms. *115*). 1st half of XIII.— Extr. Conybeare (1814; see *Ro.* xxxv. 70); Schönemann, Herbing, Zupitza (see *Bull. Soc. a. t.* 1882, 45-6); Tanner, *Die Sage von G. v. W.* (1877); Winneberger, *Über das Handschriftenverhältnis, &c.* (1888); Weyrauch, *Die mittelengl. Fassungen, &c.* (1901); Herbert in *Ro.* xxxv. 72 ff. ; Crane, *The Vogue of G. de W.* (*Publ. Mod. Lang. Ass.* xxx, 1919).—Most of the mss. are incomplete (see Winneberger, Weyrauch, and Herbert).—*416, 349, 122, 244, 79, 5, 178a, 179, 328, 308,* and a fragment in Camb. Univ. Libr., to which add *115* (*Rev. d. l. r.* lvi. 513), *316* (1,200 ll. ; cf. *Mod. Phil.* vii. 593).—*G. de W.* is a sort of legendary biography of members of the families of Wallingford and Warwick. The first part is interspersed with chivalric and courtly ideas, the second part with religious, ascetic sentiments, reminiscent of the legends of S. Eustache and S. Alexis ; cf. Ward, *Catal.* i. 471 ; Deutschbein, *Stud. zur Sagengesch. Englands,* i. 214.—*G. de W.* was utilized in the 16th century by Jean Louvet ; cf. Hibbard in *Mod. Phil.* xiii. 181 ff.

213. *Boeve de Haumtone*, 3,830 ll. in 205 laisses. 1st half of XIII. —Stimming in Bibl. Normannica vii.—*375, 393,* both incomplete.— The source is probably a northern French tale analogous to the Hamlet legend, utilized also in continental versions. Cf. Deutschbein, *Studien,* 181 ; Zenker, *Boeve-Amlethus* (1905); Jordan, *Über den B. d. H.* (1908) ; Boje, *Über d. altfranz. Roman von B. d. H.* (1909). On *B. d. H.* and Jacques de Vitry see Hibbard in *Mod. Lang. Notes,* xxxiv. On the continental versions and the mss. see Stimming in *Abhandl. Herrn Prof. Tobler dargebr.* (1895), p. 1.   See also 215.

214. *Foulques Fitz Warin*, in prose. *c.* 1258. Cf. Jordan's translation, Introd., p. xxxix.—(1) Francisque Michel, 1840. (2) T. Wright, 1855. (3) Moland and d'Héricault in *Nouvelles franç. en prose du XIVe siècle,* 1858. (4) Stevenson in *Radulphi de Coggeshale Chron.*

Angl., 1875. (5) Wood, 1911 (cf. Vising in *Jahresb. rom. Ph.* XIII. i. 244, ii. 87).—7.—The hero is a historical personage of the time of King John. The romance was translated into German by Leo Jordan, with an interesting introduction, in *Romanische Meistererzählungen* (Leipzig, 1906).

215. Other A.-N. romances are alluded to in mediaeval literature, or can be otherwise traced ; as *Aaluf*, mentioned in *Horn*, 1, 2 ; a redaction of *Horn* in assonances, of which there are traces in the rhymed *Horn*; a redaction of *Boeve* in assonances (see Stimming's ed., p. xlvii); a rhymed version of *Foulques* (*c.* 1260), of which there are traces in the prose text, e.g. page 25; ed. Moland, cf. Jordan's translation, p. xxxviii ; *Richard Cœur de Lion* (*Ro.* xxvi. 353) ; *Life of Meriadoc* (*Hist. litt.* xxx. 245) ; *Partenopeus* (Trampe Bødtker, *Partenopeus de Blois*, Christiania, 1904) ; *The Romance of the Challenge* (Kittredge, *A Study of Gawain and the Green Knight*, 1916, p. 46).

§ 2. FABLIAUX, BALLADES

216. *La housse partie*, fabliau of about 270 ll.—Extr. in *Ro.* xxxvii. 216.—*309*.—A *remaniement* of a fabliau by Bernier.

217. *Le chevalier à la corbeille*, fabliau of 264 ll.—Montaiglon and Raynaud, *Recueil gén. des Fabliaux*, ii. 183.—*78*.

218. *Les trois dames qui troverent, &c.*, fabliau of 118 ll.—Ibid. iv. 128.—*78*.—*Remaniement* of an older fabliau.

219. *Le chevalier qui faisait parler, &c.*, fabliau of 292 ll.—Ibid. vi. 198.—*78*.—*Remaniement* of a fabliau by Guerin, published ibid., p. 68.

220. *Le chevalier, sa dame et un clerc*, fabliau of 586 ll.—Ibid. ii. 215.—*244*.—*Ro.* i. 69.

221. *La gageure*, fabliau of 108 ll.—Ibid. ii. 193.—*78*.

222. *Le héron*, or *La fille mal gardée*, fabliau of 172 ll.—P. Meyer in *Ro.* xxvi. 88.—*396*.—An obscene poem, based, as P. Meyer believes, on oral tradition.

223. *Hugh of Lincoln*, ballad of 92 four-line stanzas.—(1) Francisque Michel, 1834 ; (2) F. Wolf, *Über die Lais*, 1841.—*348*.—A story of a Christian boy who was stolen in 1255 by Jews, sold and, as was believed, crucified and tortured, and whose body worked miracles and caused the tormentors to be discovered. Hume, *St. Hugh of Lincoln* (London, 1849).

224. In the *Manière de langage* (no. 389) there is inserted a translation of a novel of Boccaccio ; cf. *Ro.* xxxii. 59.—N.B. *La Bourgeoise d'Orléans*, mentioned by Louis Brandin in *Encycl. Brit.* (art. *Anglo-N. Literature*), is localized in Normandy by Bédier.

§ 3. LYRIC POETRY

225. 'De ma dame vuil chanter', five ten-line stanzas, *Ro.* iv. 375.—*138*.

226. 'Jeo m'en voys, dame', three ten-line stanzas, *Ro.* iv. 378.—*256*.

227. 'En lo sesoun qe l'erbe poynt', five eight-line stanzas with envoi.—Ibid., same ms.	These three poems have no decidedly pronounced A.-N. traits, and may belong to the XIIth century.

228. 'Le russinole voleit amer', 308 ll.; 'Lung tens ay de quer amé', five 12-line stanzas; 'Tant suy a beau sojur', three 24-line stanzas; 'Tant cum plus ai mis ma cure', five 18-line stanzas; 'Grant pesc'a ke ne chantai', three 24-line stanzas ; ' Longement me sui pené', 91 ll.; 'Quant le tens se renovele', nine 12-line stanzas.—P. Meyer, *Ro.* xv. 242.—*213.*	The last six poems, certainly by the same author, have very few A.-N. traits.

229. 'E ! dame jolyve', 45 ll.—*Ro.* xxxviii. 439.—*240.*

230. Short love-poems in *Manière de langage* (no. 389).

231. 'Ferroy chaunsoun que bien doit estre oye', two eight-line stanzas.—(1) C. Sachs, *Arch. n. Spr.* xxi. 265 ; (2) T. Wright, *Spec. Lyric Poetry*, 63.—*78.*

232. 'En une matinee me levoye', four four-line stanzas.—T. Wright, *Rel. Ant.* i. 104.—*118.*

233. ' En un verger m'en entrai', five four-line stanzas.—Francisque Michel, *Rapports*, 113.—*34.*—The love-poem published by Baker in *Rev. d. l. r.* LI. 39 is certainly not A.-N. (The form *veir*, written *veer*, but rhyming with *-ir*, is not A.-N.: cf. Tanquerey, *L'Évolution*, 430.)

234-5. Bilingual or trilingual love-poems.

234. 'En may quant dait e foil e fruit', seven four-line stanzas in French and Latin.—*Ro.* iv. 381.—*162.*

235. 'Dum ludis floribus velut lacinia', five four-line stanzas in Latin, French, and English.—T. Wright, *Spec. of Lyric Poetry*, 64.— *78.*—Other bilingual poems in mss. *264, 266.*

236. 'Amours m'ount si enchaunté', rimes équivoquées by WALTER DE BIBBESWORTH.—Extr. in *Ro.* xiii. 532.—*307.*

237. *La pleinte par entre mis sire Henry de Lacy et sire Wauter de Bybelesworthe* (Bibbesworth in Hertford), amorous tenzon of six 12-line stanzas. *c.* 1300.—Madden, *Rel. Ant.* i. 134.—*168.*

238. Love-letters in verse and prose. *c.* 1300.—Extr. *Ro.* xxxviii. 434.—*241.*

239-41. Drinking-songs.

239. 'Or i parra', six six- or eight-line stanzas with Latin refrains.— G. Paris, *Ro.* xxi. 262; many earlier editions (v. *Ro.* iv. 370, n. 1). —*15.*—A parody of *Lætabundus*, also in *Ro.* xxi. 262.

240. ' Seignors, or entendez a nus', Christmas drinking-song of six eight-line stanzas.—P. Meyer, *Rec. d'anc. textes*, 382. (On earlier editions see *Ro.* iv. 370, n. 1.)—*15.*

241. 'Hé! hé! la bone vinée', nine stanzas of different lengths.— P. Meyer in *Manière de langage* (no. 389), p. 386.—*80.*

242. *On good fare.* 'Quant voy la revenue', 144 ll.—T. Wright, *Spec. Lyric Poetry*, 13.—*78.*

243. *On friendship.* 'Cyl qe vodra oyr mes chauns', 14 eight-line stanzas.—Ed. ibid., and Stengel, *Z. f. fr. S. u. L.* xiv. 158.—*78, 192.*

244. *On the ingratitude of the great.* 'J'ay veu l'eure qe par servise', four nine-line stanzas.—Francisque Michel, *Rapports*, 112.—*34.*

245. *On the death of Simon de Montfort.* 'Chaunter m'estoit', nine

18-line stanzas with refrain.—(1) F. Wolf, *Über die Lais*, 459; (2) T. Wright, *Political Songs of England*, 125; (3) Leroux de Lincy, *Chants historiques*, i. 204.—*78*.

246. *The Song of the Church.* 'Or est acumplie', on behalf of the taxes imposed on the clergy, six ten-line stanzas. *an.* 1256.—(1) T. Wright; (2) Leroux de Lincy; (3) P. Meyer, *Ro* iv. 397 (q.v. for earlier edd.). —*31, 162*.

§ 4. DIDACTIC AND MORAL WORKS. PROVERBS

247. *Urbain le Courtois*, 146 ll. on conduct and manners. 1st half of XIII.—P. Meyer, *Ro.* xxxii. 71.—*141, 146, 163, 226, 277, 279*; diverging considerably.—P. Meyer considers the poem to be original, not based on a Latin *Urbanus*.

248. *De courtoisie*, 259 ll. 1st half of XIII.—Stengel, *Z. f. fr. S. u. L.* xiv. 151.—*182*.

249. *Corset*, about 2,400 ll. (incomplete) by ROBERT DE GRETHAM. Middle of XIII. Extr. in *Bull. Soc. a. t.* (1880), 62; *Ro.* xv. 297.—*163*. *Corset* is, as Robert says in his prologue, a sort of theological or moral encyclopaedia or 'speculum' (cf. *Miroir des domées, Miroir du monde*); for an English translation entitled *Mirrur*, see Miss Hope Emily Allen in *Mod. Phil.* xiii. 741. The extant part of this *Miroir* treats of marriage, holy orders, penance, and extreme unction. It is dedicated to Alain (cf. 71).

250. *Le secret des secrets*, 2,383 ll. by PIERRE DE PECKHAM or D'ABERNUN. Middle of XIII.—(1) In R. Steele, *Secretum Secretorum*, 1920, 287; (2) Extr. in *Ro.* xv. 288.—*370*.—This poem is a translation of the pseudo-Aristotelian *Secretum secretorum*, a moral treatise. For a prose abridgment entitled *Phisonomie*, see ms. *24*.

251. *Moral theology*, fragment of 136 ll. Middle of XIII.—Ed. P. Meyer in *Ro.* xxxv. 65.—*238*.—In this poem is inserted as an exemplum a *Life of S. Malchus*.

252. *Art of Love.* *c.* 1,000 ll. by WALTER DE HENLEY.—Extr. in Leroux de Lincy, *Le Roman de Brut*, I. lxxx.—*123*.

253. *Traitee del chevaler De.* *c.* 940 ll.—Extr. P. Meyer in *Bull. Soc. a. t.* (1880), 57.—*163*.—Religious and moral precepts for knights. According to P. Meyer original in its principal part; but the conclusion, an allegorical interpretation of the different parts of a knight's armour, is a commonplace.

254. *Dialogue between Philosophy and a Clerk.* *c.* 750 ll.—*25*.—Ward, *Catal.* ii. 728.

255. *Debate between Humility and Pride*, short poem.—*167*.

256. *On Unchastity*, 350 ll., partly a dialogue between Gilote and Johane, 1293.—Jubinal in *Nouv. Recueil*, ii. 28.—*78*.—This obscure poem ends with a moralization and a prayer.

257. *The (LX) follies*, various versions in the foll. edd. (the number of the follies varies from 32 to 60).—(1) Halliwell, *Rel. Ant.* i. 236 (32 ll.); (2) Jubinal, *Nouv. Recueil*, ii. 372 (45 ll.); (3) Heyse, *Rom. Ined.* 75 (35 ll.); (4) P. Meyer, *Jahrb. f. r. e. L.* vii. 56 (64 ll.).—*226, 84, 405, 98* (Jubinal and *Inc.* 328 give Harley 4677 instead of 4657); also *72, 182*, and *256*.— *Ro.* xv. 340; *Inc.* 328.

258–64. *Proverbs.*

258. *256*; 430 ' Proverbes de Fraunce '; ed. Leroux de Lincy, *Livre des Proverbes français*, ii. 472.

259. *4*; fol. 83 v°; 22 ll.—*71*; fol. 15 v°; 16 ll. (*Rel. Ant.* ii. 256).

260. *307*; extr. *Ro.* xiii. 532.

261. *193*; proverbs in verse.

262. *322*; cf. *Ro.* xiii. 532.—*327 a*; cf. *M. L. R.* xvi. 37.

263. *276*; *Proverbia Marie Magdalene*, rhymed; extr. *Ro.* xxxii. 40.

264. *209*; French-Latin-English proverbs in verse; extr. *Ro.* iv. 381.

265. *Proverbes de bon enseignement*, 142 four- or six-line stanzas, by NICHOLAS BOZON. End of XIII.—(1) Furnivall, *Minor Poems of the Vernon MS.* (E.E.T.S., O. S. 117, 1901); (2) Extr. *Ro.* xiii. 540; *Les Contes de Bozon*, p. xlvi; (3) Chr. Thorn (Lund, 1921).—*4, 72, 98, 111, 146, 147, 180* (incomplete), *182, 184.*—Principal source is the *Florilegium* of Sedulius Scotus; but the Bible is also drawn upon.— N.B. *Les Enseignements de Robert de Ho*, considered as A.-N. by its editor, Miss Mary Vance Young, are certainly continental; cf. *Jahresb. rom. Ph.* VI. i. 362.

§ 5. SATIRICAL AND HUMOROUS PIECES

266. *La Besturné*, 245 nonsensical verses by RICHARD. 1st half of XIII.—Stengel, *Cod. Digby 86*, 118.—*73, 151.*—A poem of the same kind as the *fatrasie*; cf. G. Paris, *La Littér. franç. au moy.-âge,* § 127.

267. *Besturné*, ' Malade sui, de joie espris ', 5 eleven-line stanzas.— P. Meyer, *Ro.* iv. 376.—*256.*

268. *La riote du monde* or *Le roi d'Angleterre et le jongleur d'Ely*, 425 ll. 2nd half of XIII.—(1) Montaiglon and Raynaud, *Recueil gén.* ii. 242; (2) Ulrich, *Z. f. rom. Ph.* viii. 275 (cf. ibid. xxiv. 112).—*78.*—A series of facetious and witty answers and wise counsels given to the king of England. The prose version of *285* probably rests on a continental original; cf. Ulrich, op. cit. 279.

269. *Fablel del gelous*, 62 ll.—Stengel, *Cod. Digby 86*, 28.—*151.*

270. *La Vie de un vallet amerous*, 344 ll., ed. ibid. from the same ms. A series of obscenities ending with a prayer.

271. *La soryte* (souris), five six-line stanzas with a refrain.—T. Wright, *Rel. Ant.* i. 107.—*118.*

272. *La Geste de Blancheflour e de Florence*, 72 six-line stanzas by BRYKHULLE.—(1) P. Meyer, *Ro.* xxxvii. 224; (2) Oulmont in *Les Débats du clerc et du chevalier* (1911).—*309.*—The author tells us that he imitated an English poem by Banastre. The subject is the question whether a *clerc* or a *chevalier* is to be preferred in love matters, a commonplace in mediaeval literature. The poem is at the same time a word-list arranged according to subjects.

273. *Melior et Ydoine*, 404 ll. on the same subject.—P. Meyer, ibid. 237.—*226.*

274. *De II chevalers torz ke plederent a Roume*, 49 ll.—Stengel, *Cod. Digby 86*, 82.—*151*.

275. Satire with the title *Chanson de geste.*—*191*.

276. *Abusive sentences* in *408* (see Koch, *Chardry's Josaphaz*, p. viii).

277-82. Poems of the praise or blame of woman.
   Praise:—

277. *Le Dit des femmes*, 114 ll. Early XIII.—(1) T. Wright, *Rel Ant.* ii. 218; (2) Jubinal, *Nouv. Recueil*, ii. 334.—*78*.—Some lines are repeated in *De Courtoisie* (No. 248).

278. *Ci comence du bounté des femmes*, 305 ll.—P. Meyer, *Ro.* xv. 316.—*226, 268*.—Cf. P. Meyer, *Ro.* viii. 334.

279. *De un valet qui soutint dames e dammaiseles*, 148 ll.—Stengel, *Cod. Digby 86*, 22.—*151*.

280. *ABC a femmes*, 30 ten-line stanzas.—T. Wright, *Spec. Lyric Poetry*, 1.—*78*.
   Blame:—

281. *Solaz de une dame*, 17 four-line stanzas.—T. Wright, *Rel. Ant.* i. 155.—*59*.

282. *De la femme et de la pye*, 13½ six-line stanzas by NICHOLAS BOZON.—(1) Jubinal, *Nouv. Recueil*, ii. 326; (2) T. Wright, *Spec. Lyric Poetry*, 107.—*78, 307*.—Bozon vilifies woman also in *Char d'Orgueil* (No. 291; cf. *Deux Poèmes de N. Bozon*, p. ix).

283-8. Political Satires:—

283. *Against Montfort's enemies*, 'Mes de Warenne ly bon quens', 13½ six-line stanzas (incomplete), 1263.—(1) F. Wolf, *Über die Lais*, 454; (2) T. Wright, *Political Songs of England*, 59; (3) Leroux de Lincy, *Chants historiques*, i. 198.—MS. in private possession; cf. Nætebus, *Die . . . Strophenformen des Altfranz.*, 154.

284. *On the Times*, 'Vulneratur karitas' .. 'Amur gist en maladie'; in Latin and French corresponding stanzas, two of 6 lines, and two of 10. End of XIII.—T. Wright, op. cit., 133.—*68*.—Cf. ibid. 251, *A Song on the Times* from the reign of Edward II, a macaronic poem in A.-N., Latin, and English (MS. 7).

285. *Ordre de bel aise*, 'Qui vodra a moi entendre', satire on the Religious Orders in England, 248 ll. End of XIII.—T. Wright, op. cit. 137.—*78*.

286. *Against Taxes*, 'Dieu, roy de magesté, ob personas trinas', 17 five-line stanzas in French and Latin. End of XIII.—T. Wright, op. cit. 182.—*78*.—There are some A.-N. lines in a Latin and English poem on Tailors in the same work, p. 51 (ms. *73*).

287. *Lettre de l'Empereur Orgueil*, 324 ll., a satire on official institutions and certain classes of people, probably by NICHOLAS BOZON. End of XIII.—(1) Wright and Halliwell, *Rel. Ant.* ii. 248; (2) Vising, in *Deux Poèmes de N. Bozon* (Göteborg, 1919).—*59, 163*.

288. *Lettre du prince des envieux*, political satire of about 30 ll.— Extr. *Ro.* xiii. 534.—*307*.

§ 6. ALLEGORY.

289. *The Four Daughters of God*, 310 ll. 1st half of XIII.—
Francisque Michel, in No. 1, p. 364.—*77, 97, 151, 233, 244.*—*Ro.*
xv. 352, xxxvii. 485, and Miss Hope Traver, *The Four Daughters of
God* (Bryn Mawr Coll. Monographs, vi. 1907). The four daughters are
Merci, Verité, Justice, Pes (Paix). The poem is based upon some lines
of Grosseteste's *Chasteau d'Amour* (No. 153). Other versions are not
A.-N. (cf. *Ro.* xxxvii. 485).

290. *Marriage of the Devil's IX daughters*, 666 ll.—P. Meyer, *Ro.*
xxix. 61.—*168, 176, 180.*— The nine daughters are Symonye, Ypocrisye,
Ravyne, Usure, Tricherie, Sacrilege, Fauce Servyse, Orgulle, Lecherye.
P. Meyer indicates some Latin texts that may be considered as
sources.

291. *Le Char d'Orgueil*, 140 four-line stanzas of 4 ll. by NICHOLAS
BOZON.—Vising in *Deux Poèmes de N. Bozon* (Göteborg, 1919).—*4*
(fragm.), *146, 229* (fragm.), *307.*—Castigation of pride and other vices,
and especially of the vanity of women (ll. 256-336). The poem seems
to be original; its contents have nothing in common with the *Lettre
de l'Empereur Orgueil* (No. 287).

§ 7. CHRONICLES.

292. *The Song of Dermot the Earl* or *The Conquest of Ireland*,
3,459 ll. (beginning and end wanting). *c.* 1225.—(1) Francisque
Michel (London), 1837; (2) Orpen (Oxford), 1892.—*135.*

293. *Crusade of Richard I*, in prose. Early XIII.—*287.*—Hardy,
Descript. Catal. ii. 523.

294. Prose chronicle from the Anglo-Saxon Heptarchy to Henry III.
—*75, 91.*— Hardy, op. cit. iii. 42.

295. *Continuation of Wace's Brut*, 1,248 ll. Middle of XIII.—
Francisque Michel in *Chroniques Anglo-Norm.* (1836) i. 65.—*40, 54*
(from l. 355).

296. *On the Erection of the town of New Ross*, 219 ll.; 1265.—
(1) Gilbert in *Facsimiles of National MSS. of Ireland* (1879), III. v,
and Append. II., also in *Account of Facsim.* (1884); (2) Madden,
Archaeologia, xxii. 315.—*71.*—Very few pronounced A.-N. traits.

297. *The Birth of Merlin*, 258 ll.—La Villemarqué, *Archives des
Missions*, 1856.—*93.*

298. *Le Livere de Reis de Brittanie et Le Livere de Reis de
Engletere*, prose chronicle from Brut to 1274. The first part is only a
very summary and uninteresting introduction to the second part.—
Glover (Rolls), 1865; the first part also by J. Koch (1886); cf.
Stengel in *Z. f. rom. Ph.* x. 278.—MSS. of both parts, *298, 375.*—
The first part is found in a great many other mss. (see Koch and
Stengel): *26, 33, 123, 126, 157, 178, 182, 183, 245, 409.*—'It is throughout little more than a translation from the known Latin historians,
generally considerably abridged, here and there words and names are
inserted. The independent value of the Chronicle rests upon these
insertions and names' (ed.). Glover conjectures that it was composed

by PETER OF ICKHAM, and that it was translated into Latin by John Pike. Glover's translation has the title *The Genealogy of the Kings of Britain (England)*, and the first part is little more than a genealogy. For other mss. that have texts of the genealogy of the Kings of England, see Hardy, *Descript. Catal.* iii. 194-6, 306, 328 ; and Ward, *Catal.* i. 594 (ms. *247*).

299. *Ordenances de les III battayles*, prose chronicle of the expedition of Edward I to Scotland in the year 1281.—Ed. in *Bannatyne Miscellany* (from ms.*139*), and in Bannatyne Club (1834, from ms. *52*) ; cf. Hardy, *D. C.* iii. 217.

300. *The Prophecies of Merlin*, prose chronicle *ex eventu* of the reigns of Henry III and Edward I. Composed during Edward's reign.—Extr. in Ward, *Catal.* i. 300, 308.—*29, 68, 92, 226, 255.*—For other political prophecies (of the XIVth cent.) see *Ro.* xxxvii. 525.

301. *On the Execution of Thomas of Turberville*, 98 ll. ; 1295 or shortly afterwards.—(1) Francisque Michel in *Eustache le Moine* (1834) ; (2) Aungier in No. 380.—*34.*—In the same MS., as in four others, there is a poem on the *Siege of Carlaveroc*, in 1300, but this poem has no A.-N. traits, a fact which at that epoch points to a French author. The poem on Turberville is preceded, [in the editions, by a letter written by him.

§ 8. NATURAL SCIENCE.

302. *La petite Philosophie*, 2,790 ll. Early XIII.—Extr. in (1) *Ro.* viii. 337, xv. 256, xxix. 73 ; (2) *Bull. Soc. a. t.* (1880) 52.—*163, 180, 213, 229, 269, 408.*—This poem treats of astrophysical matters on the basis of the *Imago Mundi* by Honorius of Autun.

303. *Calendar*, 1,200 ll. by RAUF DE LENHAM (Kent) ; 1256.—Extr. in (1) *Jahrb. f. r. e. L.* vii. 43 ; (2) by P. Meyer in *Documents manuscr.* 127 ; (3) *Ro.* xv. 286.—*145, 226, 335.*—Other Calendars (mere enumeration of days) are numerous, e. g. *201*.

304-6. Prophecies.

304. 396 ll.—Chaytor, *M. L. R.* ii. 212 (cf. *Not. et Extr.* xxxiv. 1, 236).—*315.* These prophecies are based on the moon. Similar texts occur in mss. *14, 304* (cf. *Not. et Extr.* loc. cit.).

305. 110 ll.—P. Meyer in *Ro.* xv. 323.—*189, 226.*—These Prophecies are based on the days of Christmas ; cf. *Bull. Soc. a. t.* (1883) 88.

306. *Prose Prognostica* in *198, 288, 297*, and in MSS. indicated by P. Meyer, *Not. et Extr.* xxxiv. 1. 237 ; *Ro.* xv. 323, xxxii. 101, xxxvii. 525. Cf. also mss. *264* and Cambridge, C.C.C. 37, fol. 52.

307. *Unlucky days of the year*, small pieces in verse or prose, some of which may belong to the XIIth century (cf. *Jahrb. f. r. e. L.* vii. 49 ; *Not. et Extr.* loc. cit. ; *Bull. Soc. a. t.* (1883) 94 ; Stengel, *Cod. Digby 86*, 11, 69).—*93, 151, 304, 336, 382.*

308. *Geometry* and *Geomancy*, prose treatises of the end of the XIII. —Extr. in *Ro.* xxxii. 96, 116.—*248, 281, 288.*

309-10. *On Falconry*, metrical and prose treatises.

309. 160 ll.—T. Wright, *Rel. Ant.* i. 3.0; from an unnamed ms. This poem belongs perhaps to the XIIth century.

310. Other treatises on the same subjects, one in verse, are indicated by P. Meyer in *Ro.* xiii. 506, 536, xv. 278 (cf. *Le Livre du Faucon*, Roxburghe Club, 1817).—*223, 307.*

311. *On Diseases of hunting birds*, several prose treatises.—Extr. in *Ro.* xv. 279 ff. (ms. *223*); *Cod. Digby 86*, 9 (ms. *151*).

312. *L'Art de vénerie*, prose treatise by GUILLAUME TWICH. *c.* 1300.—Sir Thomas Phillipps (1840).—Extr. in *Ro.* xiii. 505, xxxvi. 531.—*259, 307.*—On the name TWICH see *Ro.* xxxvi. 530.

313. Medical poem of nearly 2,000 ll., based on a Latin original.—Extr. (P. Meyer) in *Ro.* xxxii. 75.—*280.*

314. *La novele cirurgerie*, about 1,800 ll.—Extr. (P. Meyer) in *Ro.* xxxii. 100, xxxvii. 518.—Mss. (very much diverging) *147* (incomplete), *280.*—Rather a collection of prescriptions than a surgical treatise.

315. *The surgical treatise of Roger of Parma* in two prose translations.—Extr. (P. Meyer) in *Ro.* xxxii. 80, 91.—*280.*—Two pseudo-Hippocratic treatises in the same ms. have no A.-N. traits and are probably continental.

316. *On diseases of women*, two metrical treatises of 172 and 170 ll. in the same ms.—Extr. in *Ro.* xxxii. 90, 101.—A third poem on the same subject in the same ms. is hardly A.-N.; cf. *Ro.* xliv. 206 (continental treatises on the same subject).

317. *Euperiston*, medical prose treatise.—Extr. in P. Meyer, *Docum. manuscr.* 111.—*334.*

318. *De generaus medecines*, prose treatise in ms. *298.*

319. Medical prescriptions, some in verse, in many mss.—*139, 142, 147, 151, 191, 198, 205, 249, 251, 252, 254, 263, 280, 281, 285, 291, 334.*—Extracts from most of these mss. are to be found in *Cod. Digby 86*, 4, 7; *Ro.* xxxii. 83, 98, 113, xxxv. 579, xxxvii. 510; P. Meyer, *Docum. manuscr.* 107. Cf. M. R. James, *Catal. of the Trin. Coll. MSS.* (Cambridge), Index, sub *Receipts.*

320. *Prescriptions and formulas of exorcism* in several mss., e. g. *60, 142, 253, 278, 285, 290, 292*; cf. *Ro.* xxxii. 109, xxxv. 582 (P. Meyer). —On an incomplete version of a prose *Lapidarius* of the XIIIth century see No. 68.

§ 9. GLOSSARIES.

321. *De Utensilibus*, Latin treatise with A.-N. glosses by ALEXANDER NECKAM (d. 1217).—(1) T. Wright in *A Volume of Vocabularies*, p. 96. —*48, 108.* (2) Scheler in *Jahrb. f. r. e. L.* vii. 58.—*289, 380, 385, 393 a, 402.*

322. *Latin Glossary with A.-N. glosses. c.* 1200.—Gröber in *Festschrift zur XLVI. Versammlung deutscher Philol.*—*153.*—Another similar Glossary (unpublished) in ms. *198* (fol. 414-19).

323. *Latin-French Glossary*, 1st half of XIII.—Extr. (P. Meyer) in *Jahrb. f. r. e. L.* vii. 37 and in *Docum. manuscr.* 123.—*337.*

324. *Legal terms*, a short list. Middle of XIII. T. Wright and Halliwell, *Rel. Ant.* i. 33.—*31.*

325. *Plant names*, Latin-French-English list of the middle of the

XIII.—(1) ibid. i. 36; (2) Wright, ed. R. P. Wülcker, *Anglo-Saxon and Old English Vocab.* i. 553.—*73*.

326. *Nominale*, Latin-French.—Priebsch in *Bausteine zur rom. Philol.* (1905), 536.—*155*.

327. *Nominale sive Verbale*, 888 ll., mostly rhymed, with English translation. End of XIII.—Skeat (1906).—*219*.

§ 10. ECONOMIC LITERATURE.

328. *Les Reules Seynt Roberd*, prose treatise on agriculture by ROBERT GROSSETESTE.—Ed. see no. 329.—*60, 102 a, 104, 154, 156*.

329. *On Husbandry* (Hosebonderie), prose treatise on agriculture, cattle-breeding, etc., by WALTER DE HENLEY. (1) Lacour in *Bibl. de l'École d. Chartes*, 1856; (2) Miss Elizabeth Lamond, together with No. 328 (for the Royal Historical Society, 1890). Mss., 21 in number (see ed. Lamond, p. xxiii), principally in the British Museum, Oxford, and Cambridge. The Lacour ed. is from a Paris ms., the Lamond ed. from ms. *216*. The best mss. are Cambr. Univ. Libr., Dd. vii. 6 and Dd. vii. 14. As the mss. differ very much, some may be considered as new redactions. One of these redactions has been published by Miss Lamond from *105, 207, 230, 327, 354*.—A *Housebondrea* is also inserted in *Liber Horn* (No. 343). Other works on *Hosebonderie* are indicated in the article *Henley, Walter of*, in *D.N.B.* It is also stated there that Grosseteste is not the author of this *Hosebonderie*, nor the translator of an English text (cf. J. Murray, *Le Château d'Amour*, 19). Cf. also ms. *251*.

330. *Seneschaucie*, prose treatise on the management of an estate.— Miss E. Lamond, together with 329.- ·Seven mss., in London and Cambridge ; see ed.

§ 11. LAWS AND PUBLIC DOCUMENTS.

Laws and Public Documents have been published in a great number of collections, of which the most important will be cited below, in this and the following chapters. See also the works of Scargill-Bird and Gross, cited p. 102 ; and Tanquerey, *L'Évol.* pp. xx-xxii, and *Recueil de Lettres*, pp. viii ff.

331. *Laws of William the Conqueror* or *Leis Willelme*, the original of which probably dates from the first half of the XIIth century and is recognizable under the later features of the ms.—(1) Matzke in *Collection de textes pour servir à l'étude de l'histoire* (with an historical introduction by Ch. Bémont, 1899); (2) Liebermann in *Die Gesetze der Angelsachsen* (1903), i. 492. Earlier editions are indicated by Matzke (cf. *Literaturbl. f. g. u. r. Ph.* xxii. 120).—*332*, and some passages in *Arch. f. n. Spr.* cvi. 113, Ingulf's History (cf. Liebermann in *Arch. f. n. Spr.* cvi. 113). The A.-N. text is the original of the Latin texts (cf. Liebermann, loc. cit. See also *Arch. f. n. Spr.* cvii. 134, and *Ro.* xxix. 153).

332. *Wilhelmi Articuli.* Original 1192-3 ; ms. of about 1300.— Liebermann in (1) *Z. f. rom. Ph.* xix. 82, and (2) *Die Gesetze der Angelsachsen*, i. 488.—*216*.

333. *Britton*, an extract of English laws, probably made by a lawyer named BRITTON (cf. Introduction of the edition). End of XIII. Ed. Nichols, 1865, 2 vols.—Extr. in Toynbee, *Specimens of Old French*, p. 239.—Translation by Nichols and by Kelham (1762). Twenty-six mss. indicated in the edition, pp. xlix-liii, mostly in London and Cambridge; the oldest ms. is *132, c.* 1300, on which the edition is based. Cf. Gross, *Sources and Literature of Engl. Hist.* 314.

334. *The Coronation act of William 1st* in A.-N. translation of the beginning of the XIIIth century.—Liebermann in the *Transactions of the Royal Historical Society*, 1894. Cf. *On Coronation* in ms. Cambridge C.C.C. 20.

335. *Fœdera, Conventiones, Litteræ, et cujuscunque generis Acta Publica*, ed. Thomas Rymer and Robert Sanderson. 20 vol., 1704-35, &c. The first Anglo-N. document is of the date 1256.

336. *Statutes of the Realm*, 1st ed. 1810, 3rd ed. 1888.—14 vol. A.-N. statutes, 1258-1488.

337. *A Statute of Edward I* in *Z. f. rom. Ph.* xvii. 279.

338. *Chronica Monasterii S. Albani*, ed. Riley. 7 vol. (Rolls), 1863-76. A.-N. documents from 1259. ·

339. *Annales Monastici*, ed. Luard, 5 vol. (Rolls), 1864-69. A.-N. documents from 1259.

340. *Liber Rubeus de Scaccario*, ed. Hall. 3 vol., 1896. A.-N. documents from 1266.

341. *Lettres de Rois, Reines et autres personnages*, ed. Champollion-Figeac, Paris, 1839-47. A.-N. letters from 1272.

342. *Rotuli Parliamentorum*, ed. Cole, 1844. A.-N. documents from 1278.

343. *Munimenta Gildhallæ Londoniensis*, ed. Riley, 1859-62. 1. *Liber Albus.* 2. *Liber Custumarum.* 3. Translation and Glossary. A 4th part, *Liber Horn*, probably compiled by ANDREW HORN in 1311, is still unpublished. This work contains many A.-N. texts (from 1280) concerning election of magistrates, legal procedures, commerce, trade, wills, &c.— Mss. *137* and Br. M. Cott. Claud. D 11.—A copy of *Les Estatuz de Lundres oue les Avoystemens de novels Estatuz* is in ms. *66.*

344. *The Acts of the Parliament of Scotland*, ed. Thomson & Innes, 1814 ff., &c. A.-N. statutes from the XIIIth century.

345. *Historic and Municipal Documents of Ireland*, ed. Gilbert, 1870, containing *Les Leys et les Usages de la cyté de Diueline* (p. 240) and *Grievances of the common folk of Dublin* (p. 359).—*344.*

346. *Annales Londonienses*, ed. Stubbs, 1882. Contains a *Chronicle of the Reigns of Edw. I and Edw. II.* In part an abridgement of the *Flores Historiarum*, perhaps written by ANDREW HORN (d. 1328).

347. *Monumenta Juridica. The Black Book of the Admiralty*, ed. Travers Twiss, 1871-76. 4 vol. A collection of laws relating to the navy. A.-N. documents from 1291 (i. 380, ii. 1, iii. 4).—Numerous mss. of the XIVth century in the Admiralty archives of Whitehall.

348. *Documents illustrative of the History of Scotland, 1286-1306*, ed. J. Stevenson, 1870, 2 vol. In vol. i A.-N. from the end of the XIIIth century ; in vol. ii from the XIVth century.

349. *Year Books of the Reign of King Edward I.*, ed. Horwood,

5 vol. (Rolls), consist of reports of cases of the XIIIth century.—Mss. mostly in Lincoln's Inn and the Temple, others among the Addit. mss. of the Brit. Mus.—'The year books, 1292–1535, [are] so called because there was one for each regnal year. They are anonymous law reports, written in French, containing the discussions of the judges and counsel on the points of law, and the grounds of judgment in important cases tried before the royal justices either at Westminster or in eyre... Much legal and constitutional history still lies buried in the year books, a good edition of which has long been an urgent want.' (Gross, *Sources and Literature of English History*.) 'They should be our glory, for no other country has anything like them, they are our disgrace, for no other country would have so neglected them' (Pollock and Maitland, *English Law*). As appears by the dates given by Gross, not many law reports in A.-N. date from the XIIIth century. It is therefore of importance to point out that there are such reports in the ms. *286* (Cambridge Trin. Coll., O. 3. 45, fol. 17, 22 (27)).

350. *Registrum Malmesburiense*, ed. Brewer, 2 vol. In vol. i, besides a short 'brieth,' there are some A.-N. statutes of Westminster (pp. 201–38).

351. *La Court de Baron (Curia Baronis)*.—F. W. Maitland and W. P. Baildon, *The Court Baron* (Selden Soc., 1891). 7 mss., see edition.—A poem of about 500 ll. in mss. Harley 5213, Addit. 19559 (cf. *Inc.* 54).

N.B.—Numerous collections of official Documents of all sorts are quoted and discussed by Tanquerey in *Recueil de Lettres Anglo-Françaises* (Paris, 1916), p. xii.—In the same work (p. v) is to be found a report of the rich collections of official Letters preserved in the Public Record Office of London.

Extracts from many of these collections are given in the same work.

IV. THE FOURTEENTH CENTURY

A. Religious Literature

§ 1. THE BIBLE.

352. *The Anglo-Norman Bible*, prose translation incomplete.— Extr. in Berger, *La Bible*, 231–36.—*1* (from Genesis to Tobit), *346* (ends in Epist. to Hebr.), *355* (Acts of Apostles).—' Un texte déplorable au point de vue de la pureté du langage, mais bien intéressant comme témoin de l'idiome parlé à cette époque chez nos voisins' (Berger, 237). Ms. *1* contains Prologues in a very corrupt language mixed with English words.

353. *Genesis*, about 2,200 ll.; incomplete at the beginning and end. 1st half of XIV.—Extr. *Ro.* xxxvi. 188.—MS. *79*.—The glossed Apocalypse that P. Meyer published for the Soc. a. t. 1901 is probably of Continental origin, though it was copied many times in England. The *Books of Maccabees*, published by Görlich (1888) in *Rom. Bibl.*, are also probably Continental (cf. *Jahresb. rom. Ph.* i. 377).

§ 2. ALLEGORY.

354. *The seven things that God hates*, 99 ll. in 8 laisses.—Early XIV. —P. Meyer in *Ro*. xxxvii. 212.—*309.*—A paraphrase of Proverbs.

355. *The Passion of Christ*, or *Du Roy qui avoit une Amie*, 50 four-line stanzas by NICHOLAS BOZON. Early XIV.—(1) Jubinal, *Nouv. Recueil*, ii. 309; (2) T. Wright in *The Chronicle of Langtoft*, ii. 426.— *29, 307.*—Cf. *Ro*. xiii. 506 and *Les Contes . . de N. Bozon*, p. xli.

356. *Coment le fiz Deu fu arme en la croyz*, 18 four-line stanzas, probably by NICHOLAS BOZON. Early XIV.—Extr. (P. Meyer) in *Ro*. xiii. 530.—*307.*

357. *La Plainte d'Amour*, 169 six-line stanzas, probably by NICHOLAS BOZON. 1312 or shortly afterwards (cf. ed. iv. 21).—Vising (Göteborg, 1905-7, in *Göteborgs Högskolas Årsskrift*).—*60, 180, 226, 279, 307.*— Certain passages are reminiscent of the *Roman de Carité*, by the Renclus de Moiliens, others of the *Vers de la Mort*, by Helinand ; the starting-point is the Bulla *Exivi de Paradiso* (6 May, 1312); but on the whole the poem seems to be original. It has stylistic merits, which has inclined Tanquerey to doubt BOZON'S authorship (*L'Évol.* p. xvi, *n.* 2).

B. Secular Literature

§ 1. LYRIC POETRY.

358. *On the death of Edward I*, ' Seignurs, oiez pur Dieu le grant,' 1 ten-line stanza, 9 eight-line stanzas, 1307.—T. Wright in *The Political Songs of England*, 241.—*226.*

359. *De bone femme la bounté*, 39 six-line stanzas by NICHOLAS BOZON. Early XIV.—P. Meyer in *Les Contes moralisés de N. B.*, p. xxxiii.—*307.*

359a. *De le roi Edward le fiz roi Edward, le Chanson qe il fist mesmes*, 15 eight-line stanzas.—P. Studer in *M. L. R.* xvi. 34 ff.—Ms. *327 a. Chastel de leal amour* and a *Diffinission de Amur* in the same ms. are hardly A.-N.

360. *Cinkante Balades*, love poems by JOHN GOWER. The 3 first stanzas of each *balade* have 8 ll., the fourth 4 ll. Two dedications open the series, put together by Gower in 1399.—(1) Stengel in *Ausg. u. Abh.* lxiv ; (2) G. C. Macaulay in *The Complete Works of J. G.*— *329.*

§ 2. DIDACTIC AND MORAL WORKS.

361-6 are probably by NICHOLAS BOZON and of the beginning of the XIVth century.

361. *Desputeison de l'ame et du corps*, 65 six-line stanzas.—Stengel in *Z. f. rom. Ph.* iv. 74 (cf. ibid., 365, 585).—Mss., showing much divergence, *41, 96, 182* (with a Prologue), *307*. Cf. *Inc.* 393.

362. *On Denaturesse* (friendliness), short poem attributed by the copyist to *Nich. Boioun* (BOZON).—Extr. (P. Meyer) in *Ro*. xiii. 508.—*307.*

363. *Peynes e joies*, about 100 ll.—Extr. ibid. p. 523, and same ms.

364. *On moral life*, ' Un prodom en compaignie,' short poem.—Extr. ibid. p. 527, and same ms.

365. *Parable of the demi-ami*, 37 six-line stanzas (incomplete), probably by BOZON; cf. *Jahresb. rom. Ph.* x. ii. 108.—P. Meyer, *Ro.* xxxv. 50.—*143*.

366. *De l'Yver et de l'Esté*, 277 ll., partly in stanzas.—Jubinal, *Nouv. Recueil*, ii. 40.—*78*.

367. *On Chess.* Two treatises in verse and prose, probably from the same Latin original (cf. Ward, *Catal.* i. 594).—*11, 54 a.*—Extr. in H. J. R. Murray, *History of Chess* (1913), 583 ff.

368. *Les Contes moralisés de* NICOLE BOZON.—Miss Lucy Toulmin Smith and P. Meyer (Soc. a. t., 1889).—*129, 307.*—Schofield, *English Literature*, 118, says of the author : ' an industrious populariser of clerical learning at the beginning of the fourteenth century, and a story-teller sometimes of considerable skill '. B.'s sources are ancient authors on the *proprietates rerum*, such as Bartholomaeus Anglicus among others ; collections of *Exempla* and *Fabulae*; cf. editor's Introd. and P. W. Harry, *A Comparative Study of the Aesopic Fable in N. B.* (Cincinnati, 1903).—This work, with the *Plainte d'Amour*, is Bozon's best work : see Vising's Introd. to the *Plainte*.

369. *Mirour de l'omme*, about 30,000 ll. on sin, virtue, the Church, the State, the holy Virgin, &c., by JOHN GOWER. 1376-9.—G. C. Macaulay in *The Complete Works of J. G.—237.*—For Gower's language see editor's Introd. and Tanneberger, *Sprachliche Untersuchung der franz. Werke J. G.'s* (1910).—Miss Elfreda Fowler, *Une Source française des Poèmes de Gower* (Macon, 1905), gives, principally on the basis of Macaulay's Introduction, an account of Gower's life and of his three great poems. One finds that Gower's *Mirour de l'omme* is very close to Frère Lorens' *Somme le Roi*, and still closer to a *Mireour du Monde*, in great part unpublished. This work probably rests upon two older *summae*; a version of one of these was made use of by Gower's contemporary Chaucer for the *Parson's Tale.*

370. *Traitié pour essampler les amantz mariez*, 55 seven-line stanzas by JOHN GOWER.—(1) Stengel (with No. 360) ; (2) Macaulay (with No. 369).—Ten mss., see Macaulay, op. cit., p. lxxxv.

§ 3. SATIRICAL PIECES.

371. *Traillebastoun*: ' Talent me prent de rymer e de geste fere ', 23 four-line stanzas and 1 six-line. 1305.—T. Wright in *Political Songs of England*, 231.—*78.*—*Trailbastoun* is, according to the *Oxford Engl. Dict.*, 'one of a class of violent evil-doers in the reign of Edward I, who, as brigands or hired ruffians, bludgeoned, maltreated, and robbed the king's lieges. . . . Thence contextually applied also to the ordinances issued against them, and to the inquisitions, trials, courts, and justices appointed for their suppression.' This poem is a satire on those ordinances. Cf. *Archaeologia*, xl. 89.

372. *On the transgression of Magna Charta*: ' L'en peut fere et defere,' French and English poem. 1311.—Ibid., 253, from the Auchinleck ms. (*334 a*).

N. B. On a Latin and English satire with A.-N. words inserted, see No. 284.

§ 4. CHRONICLES.

373. *Continuation of Le Livere de Reis de Engletere* (No. 298) to 1306, called 'Wroxham Continuation' (*298*), and to 1326, called 'Sempringham Continuation' (*409*), both published by Glover together with No. 298.

374. *The Saxon and Norman Kings* down to Edward I. Early XIV.—*186, 244.*—Hardy, *Descr. Catal.* iii. 198.

375.—*Petit Brut*, prose chronicle down to 1310, compiled by RAUF DE BOHUN from No. 298. Early XIV.—*69.*—P. Meyer in *Bull. Soc. a. t.* (1878) 111.

376. *Polistorie*, down to 1313, by JOHN OF CANTERBURY. Early XIV.—Extr. in (1) *Hist. litt.* xxviii. 481 (G. Paris), (2) *Publ. Mod. Lang. Assoc.* xviii. 90 (Fletcher).—*30, 38, 65, 403 a.* G. Paris, op. cit.

377. *Chronicle of Pierre de Langtoft*, from the destruction of Troy to 1307, 10,189 ll. 1st half of XIV.—T. Wright (Rolls), 1866.—*20, 22* (increased by 672 ll.), *29, 123* (fragm.), *125, 159* (incomplete; cf. *Bull. Soc. a. t.*, 1878, 140), *168* (fragm.), *186, 226, 356.* Moreover, two mss. cited *Revue crit.*, 1867 II. 198; cf. *Bibl. de l'Ecole des Chartes*, 5, ii. 278.—Behrenroth, *Das Verhältn. des 1. Teiles der Reimchr. P. de L. zu seinen Quellen* (1912); Tischbein, *Über Verfasser u. Quellen des 2. Teiles der altfr. Reimchr. P. de L.* (1913), where the different sources are examined. They are for Part I principally Gotfrid of Monmouth, for Part II most of the earlier Latin Chronicles of England.—Pierre was a North-Englishman (Behrenroth, p. 3). His work was translated into English by Robert of Brunne, who completed his work on May 15, 1338 (see Thümmig in *Anglia*, xiv. 1).

378. *Brute of England* in many versions and mss. See B ie, *Geschichte und Quellen der mittelengl. Prosachronik The Br. of E. oder The Chronicles of England* (Marburg, 1905). Mostly unpublished.

a. to 1272. Extr. in *Bull. Soc. a. t.* (1878) 115 (P. Meyer)—*32, 113, 295, 361, 373*;

b. to 1307. Extr. ibid. 106—*226*;

c. to 1333—*50, 56, 114, 185, 234*;

d. Same version with a metrical prologue 'Des graunz jaianz ki primes conquistrent Bretaigne', 562 ll. publ. by Jubinal, *Nouv. Recueil*, ii. 354 (*57*), and Francisque Michel in *Gesta Regum Brit.* (1862), 900.—Extr. in *Bull. Soc. a. t.* (1878) 117 (from the chronicle)—*28, 88, 108, 109, 124, 127, 133, 178, 195, 227, 296, 342, 358* (introduction completely different), a Dublin- ms. (cf. *Ro.* xliv. 135), and a ms. Brie. A great many mss. are incomplete;

e. Same version modified, with the metrical prologue—*58, 160*;

f. to 1398, with a prose version of the prologue. Extr. in *Bull. Soc. a. t.* (1878) 132—*190*;

g. More detailed continuation to 1307, without the prologue. Extr. ibid. 125—*217*;

h. Detailed continuation to 1333, with a prose version of the prologue—*19, 21, 27, 55, 108, 128, 140, 232, 343, 357, 391, 392*;

i. A partial *remaniement*; extr. in *Bull. Soc. a. t.* (1878) 142—*23* (to 1328), *106* (to 1181). Cf. Brie, p. 31.

On these and other minor French chronicles 'Bruts', see also Robert Huntington Fletcher, *Studies and Notes in Philology and Literature*, vol. x (1906, Harvard University) 209, and cf. *Inc.* 443, 'Vous qui desirez a savoir' (ms. Harley, 1808), and ms. *297*, p. 15.

379. *Les Cronicles qe frere N. Trevet escript &c.* (the full title in *Dictionary of National Biography*), from the Creation to 1313.—Extr. in (1) Spelman, *Concilia*, i. 104; (2) Brock, *The Life of Constance* (Chaucer Soc., 1872).—*130, 158, 171, 174, 203, 287*; on a ms. at Wrest Park see *Hist. Mss. Commission*, 2nd Report, p. 6.—The author, NICHOLAS TREVET, or TRIVET, was a Dominican friar who taught in the schools of Oxford and died in 1328. He wrote many Latin works, among them *Historia ab orbe condito usque ad suum tempus*, of which the French Chronicle is a translation. It is supposed that Chaucer took the subject of *The Man of Law's Tale* from this chronicle. Cf. *D. N. B.*, Brock, op. cit., and Hardy, *Descr. Cat.* iii. 297, 349 (an Arundel ms.).

380. *Croniques de London*, 1260-1344, in prose. Mid-XIV.— Aungier (Camden Soc., 1844).—*53*.—Translations by Riley, 1863, and by Goldsmid, 1885.

381. *On the Meeting of the Kings of England and France in 1346*, prose chronicle of Mid-XIV.—*208*.

382. *Scalacronica*, prose chronicle of England and Scotland from the Creation to 1362, by THOMAS GRAY OF HETON (whose arms bore a *scala*). Shortly after 1362.—J. Stevenson (Maitland Club, 1836, from year 1066 to 1362; beginning as Append.); extr. in the *Chronicle of the Picts*, ed. Skene (p. 194).—*248, 262*.—This chronicle is principally based on Bede, Higden, and other well-known authors, but also contains useful information concerning the reigns of Edward I and Edward II. An English translation was published by Sir Herbert Maxwell in 1907.

N.B.—*The Life of the Black Prince*, by SIR JOHN CHANDOS, formerly considered to be A.-N., has been proved to be continental by Miss Mildred K. Pope in her excellent edition (1910). Only some lines at the end can be ascribed to the A.-N. scribe.

§ 5. NATURAL SCIENCE.

383. *On the 12 Waters*, prose treatise.—Extr. (P. Meyer) in *Ro.* xxxvii. 522.—*147*.

384. *Culinary Receipts* in prose.—P. Meyer in *Bull. Soc. a. t.* (1893) 49.—*7*.—Other receipts of the same kind are quoted ibid.

385. *On Wine*, prose treatise with alliterations ('vin bon, bel et blanc', &c.).—P. Meyer, *Ro.* xi. 574.—*8, 90*.—T. Wright, *Rel. Ant.* i. 273, ii. 29.

§ 6. GLOSSARIES AND GRAMMARS.

386. *A Treatise on the French language* (with special treatment of homophones), about 850 ll., by WALTER DE BIBBESWORTH. *c.* 1300.— (1) T. Wright in *A Volume of Vocabularies*, p. 142 (*93, 100*); (2) Wright and Halliwell, *Rel. Ant.* ii. 78 (*226*).—*10* (fragm.), *43, 62* (fragm.), *67*,

93, 99, 100, 182 (fragm.), *187, 226, 256, 283, 306, 307.*—De la Rue, *Essais*, i. 283, Michel, *Rapports*, 1838, p. 14; Palsgrave, *L'Esclaircissement*, 1852, p. 27; P. Meyer, *Rec. d'Anciens Textes*, 360; *Ro.* xiii. 502, xxxii. 44; C. T. Onions in *Times Lit. Supp.*, 1922, Apr. 6, p. 228 (notice of ms. Bodl. 39).

387. *Orthographia Gallica*, Latin prose treatise with A.-N. examples and rules. 1st half of XIV.—Stürzinger (Altfr. Bibl. 1884).—*86* (contains other grammatical or lexicographical pieces), *136, 204, 219*.

388. *Tractatus Orthographie Gallicane*, Latin prose treatise with A.-N. words and phrases, by COYFURELLY. End of XIV.—Stengel in *Z. f. fr. S. u. L.* i. 16.—*187.*—Another Latin treatise on conjugation *Ro.* xxxii. 66 (XIII. cent.).

389. *Maniere de Langage*, phrase-book by COYFURELLY. 1396.— P. Meyer (1873, a short continuation by Stengel in *Z. f. fr. S. u. L.* i. 6).—*80, 107, 187, 214, 306.*—P. Meyer in *Ro.* xv. 262, xxxii. 59. In most mss. of the *Maniere* there is inserted an A.-N. translation of a novel of Boccaccio (cf. No. 224).

390. *Aprise de nurture*, 240 ll.—*141* (cf. *Inc.* 39).

391. Treatises on A.-N. Epistolography, with Examples (partly of the XV. cent.).—W. Uerkvitz (Greifswald, 1898).—The manuscript collections are the following :—

219, letters from 1327-40, based on formularies drawn up by a teacher THOMAS SAMPSON ;

107, letters of the first half of the XIV. cent. ;

86, letters from 1396-99 ;

187, letters from 1400-8 ;

80, letters from the first quarter of the XV. cent.

392. Similar formularies with Latin text in original are in ms. *277* (Trin. Coll. Cambridge, B. 14. 40, cf. M. R. James's *Catal.*).

§ 7. Laws and Public Documents.

On legal writers, &c., see Gross, *Sources and Literature of English History*, 312 ff. To the series cited under No. 331 ff. may be added :—

393. Three official *Letters* on the suzerainty of Scotland, translated into verse by PIERRE DE LANGTOFT. Early XIV.—Ed. as Append. I to the *Chronicle of Langtoft* (No. 377).—*22, 309.* Cf. *Ro.* xxxvii. 210 (P. Meyer).

394. *La Somme appellé Mirroir des Justices*, by ANDREW HORN. *c.* 1300. Printed London, 1642, and often since, e. g. in Houard, *Loix Anglo-normandes* (Rouen, 1776), vol. iv.

395. *The Oak Book of Southampton* (so called because of its binding). The oldest part, Chs. iv. and v, is written about 1300, other parts much later.—P. Studer, Southampton, 1910-11. Vol. i contains an Introduction and the Anglo-French Ordinances of the ancient Guild Merchant of Southampton ; vol. ii, a fourteenth-century version of the mediaeval Sea-Laws known as the Rolls of Oleron ; vol. iii., Notes on the Anglo-French Dialect of Southampton, Glossary and Indexes.—*325*.

396. *Year Books of the Reign of King Edward II.*, ed. F. W. Maitland (Selden Soc.), 1903 &c.

397. *Year Books of the Reign of King Edward III.*, ed. Horwood and Pike (Rolls Ser.), 1866 &c.

398. *The Percy Chartulary*, i. (from 1241 to 1377).—Ed. Surtees Soc., 1911 (No. 120).

399. *Wills* are frequent in A.-N. from the middle of the XIVth century, e.g. from 1347 in the *Testamenta Eboracensia* and *Wills and Inventories* published for the Surtees Soc. (Nos. 2, 4, 26).

V. THE FIFTEENTH CENTURY

§ 1. GRAMMAR.

400. *Donait François*, prose treatise by JOHN BARTON. *c.* 1400.—Stengel in *Z.f.fr.S.u. L.* i. 25.—*187.*—In the same ms. are to be found tables of conjugation and reading exercises. The treatise *Petit Livre pour enseigner les enfantz*, published by Stengel together with the *Donait*, has few A.-N. traits.

401. *Femina* (so named 'quia sicut femina docet infantem loqui maternam sic docet iste liber iuvenes rethorice loqui gallicam'), about 600 four-line stanzas, consisting throughout of two lines of French alternating with two lines of the English equivalent. *c.* 1400.—Extr. in Hickes, *Thesaurus*, 1705, i. 154-5 ; ed. W. A. Wright (1909).—*277.*

402. *Dialogues.* 1415.—P. Meyer, *Ro.* xxxii. 49.—*107, 214, 277.*

403. *Inn Dialogues* and *Magniere de language.*—Extr. in Stürzinger, *Orthographia Gallica*, p. xv.—*231.*

N.B.—Later *Dialogues*, printed during the XVth century, are hardly to be reckoned as part of A.-N. literature. Some Dialogues of the kind are quoted by Stürzinger, op. cit., p. xv, e.g. Caxton's *Book for Travellers* and Wynken's *Lytell Treatyse*.

§ 2. LAWS AND PUBLIC DOCUMENTS.

404. *The York Memorandum Book*, i. 1376-1419 ; ii. 1388-1493.—Surtees Soc., 1911, 1914 (some A.-N. texts).

Other documents of the XVth century are to be found in nos. 335, 395, &c.

N.B. *Roundels and Ballads* by WILLIAM DE LA POLE, DUKE OF SUFFOLK, cannot be classed as A.-N.

VI. LATER LEGAL LITERATURE (*Law French*)

1. *Tenures*, by THOMAS LITTLETON (d. 1481), first printed 1475 ; numerous edd. Cf. Gross, p. 316.—Extr. in Toynbee, *Specimens of Old French*, 375.

2. *La Graunde Abridgement*, 1514.

3. *La Novel Natura Brevium*, 1534.

4. *L'Office et auctoryte de Justyces de peas*, 1538.

5. *L'Office de Viconts, Bailiffes, Escheators, &c.*, 1538.—All four by ANTHONY FITZHERBERT (d. 1538).

6. *Perutilis Tractatus*, by JOHN PERKINS (d. 1545).

7. *Les Plees del Coron*, by WILLIAM STANFORD (d. 1558), 1560.

8. *La Graunde Abridgement*, by ROBERT BROOKE or BROKE (d. 1558). 1568, &c.—An extract is *Ascuns Novell Cases de les ans et* *temps le Roy Henry VIII, Edward VI et la Roygne Marie escrie ex la grand Abridgement.* 1578, &c.

9. *Les Comentaries, ou les Reportes de Edmunde Plowden, vn apprentice de le comen Ley, de dyuers cases esteantes matters en ley, & de les Argumentes sur yceux, en les temps des Raygnes le Roye Edwarde le size, le Roigne Mary, le Roy & Roigne Philipp & Mary, & le Roigne Elisabeth,* 1571, &c.

10. *Les Quæres del Monsieur Plowden.* Sine anno.

11. *Le Digest des Briefes originals, et des Choses concernant eux,* by SIMON THELOALL. 1579.

12. *Reports,* 1585, &c.

13. *Cy ensuont ascuns Novels Cases,* 1585.

14. *Vn Abridgement de Touts les Cases,* 1609 = all three by JAMES DYER (d. 1582).

15. *Reports,* by EDMUND ANDERSON (d. 1605). 1653–64.

16. *Les Reports de Edward Coke,* Thirteen Parts, of which the first eleven are in French with the depositions in Latin. 1600–18, &c.

17. *Le Reading del Mon Seignior Coke sur . . lestatute de Finibus Levatis,* 1662, both by SIR EDWARD COKE or COOK (d. 1634).

18. *Cases, Reports, &c.,* by GULIELME DALISON or DALLSON, 1609, and 1689 in *Reports des divers Cases adjugez en la Court de Common Bank en les Regnes Mary et Elizabeth.*

19. *Reports* by JOHN DAVIES (d. 1626). 1615. (English translation 1762.)

20. *L'Authoritié et Jurisdiction des Courts de la Maiestié de la Roygne : Nouelment collect & composé, per R. Crompton del milieu Temple Esquire, Apprentice del Ley.* 1594, 1637.

21. *Reports and Cases* by JOHN POPHAM (d. 1607). 1656. Only the 1st Part in French.

22. *Un Abridgment des Plusieurs Cases et Resolutions del Common Ley, Alphabeticalment digest desouth severall Titles.* 1668.

23. *Les Reports de divers Cases en le Court del' Banke le Roy, en le Temps del' Reign de Roy Jaques.* 1675, &c.

24. *Un Continuation,* 1676.—All three by HENRY ROLLE (d. 1656).

25. *Les Reports de Gulielme Benloe Serjeant del Ley, des divers pleadings et cases en le Court del Comon-bank, en le several Roignes de les tres hault & excellent Princes, le Roy Henry VII, &c.* 1689.— BENLOE or BENDLOWES died in 1584.

26. *Reports* by THOMAS JONES (d. 1692). 1695.

27. *Reports* by CRESWELL LEVINZ (d. 1701). 1702 (with Engl. translation).

28. *Reports of Cases* by EDWARD LUTWYCHE (d. 1709). 1704 (French and Latin).

There are extant also unpublished lectures on statutes, &c., in Law French held at the Inns of Court or at Oxford. The lecturers named in the mss. are: Deynshyll, Fitzherbert, Rob. Catlin, Ambrose Giberte, Edm. Plowden, Waltham, Robins, Selwin, Waintworth (Wentworth), Ayloffe, Jeffries, Eyre, Puck, Escott, Chibborne, Hadd, Th. Nichols, all of the XVIth or the beginning of the XVIIth cent. The mss. are: Oxford, Exeter Coll. 108, 163, 173, all of the XVIIth cent.

VII. ANGLO-NORMAN VERSIFICATION

§ 1. Number of Syllables

The fundamental principles of French verse are syllabism and rhyme, with accent and caesura as accessory elements. This system of versification was brought over to England by the Normans, and it is the form adopted in most of the Anglo-Norman poems of the twelfth century. The following numbers in Part II of this work belong to this class. In some of them only slight alterations of manuscript readings are needed in order to arrive at metrical correctness :—

Nos. 4, 6, 8, 10–12 (for No. 10, see below), 14, 15, 22, 25, 27, 29, 30 (in all probability, cf. ed.), 32–36, 39, 41, 44, 47, 54, 58, 60, 64–7, and the lyric poems No. 228, of the thirteenth century.

From the middle of the twelfth century, the pronunciation of atonic *e* and the rules of elision and hiatus begin to be uncertain. The consequence is that many verses may be considered as 'correct' from an Anglo-Norman point of view, though in French they are irregular. Geffrey Gaimar is the first author whose verses are marked by such irregularities. His example is followed, in the twelfth century, in Nos. 9, 13, 16–18, 35, 37, 40, 42, 43, 53, 55, 57, 70, and in poems of the thirteenth and fourteenth centuries, for instance in Angier's poems (No. 108), and in No. 109.

Later, with the increasing changes in pronunciation and the neglect of French rules, the decline of versification was continued to such a point that a poet was often satisfied if he wrote lines of approximatively the same length. The earliest writer to exhibit metrical features of this kind is Jourdain Fantosme. The kind of versification we find in his *Chronicle* (No. 62) is found also in some other poems of the twelfth century : Nos. 23, 28, 45, 46, 51, 52, and in most of the poems of the thirteenth and fourteenth centuries.

This development of French versification in England may be compared with that which took place in another branch of French literature produced on a foreign soil, the Franco-Italian. An example can be seen in the *Aspremont* of the Paris MS., Bibl. Nat. f. fr. 1598, published by Meyer-Lübke in *Z. f. rom. Ph.* x; see his remarks, ibid., p. 54.

The Anglo-Norman poets often confess their lack of skill in French prosody in addition to their general ignorance of the language. Passages to this effect have been quoted on pp. 26, 27. They are in marked contrast with the confident declarations of some continental writers. Thus Garnier de Pont-Sainte-Maxence, in his *Vie de St. Thomas* of the late twelfth century, says:

> Ainc mes mieldre romanz ne fu fez ne trovez:
> A Cantorbire fut et fet et amendez;
> N'i a mis un sul mot qui ne seit veritez.
> Li vers est d'une rime en cinc clauses coplez.
> Mis languages est buens; car en France fui nez.

Of similar date is the poem on the First Crusade published by Paul Meyer in *Romania*, v, pp. 8 ff., in which the author says (ll. 31–2):

> Ore vous comencerai l'estoire bien rimée,
> Tute faite par metre sanz sillabe fausée.

Another instance may be quoted from the romance of *Orson de Beauvais* (13th century):

> Seignours, oez chançon dont li ver sunt bien fait.
> (Michel, *Rapports*, 1838, p. 49.)

The view of Anglo-Norman versification adopted in this chapter has been stated in many places before. For example, Gaston Paris says, in the Introduction to *L'Évangile de Nicodème*, p. xlvii: 'Nous ne croyons pas à une métrique anglo-normande particulière, mais nous sommes bien convaincus que beaucoup de rimeurs anglo-normands, surtout à l'époque où a été composée notre version [second half of the thirteenth century], n'avaient dans la tête qu'un rythme vague.' Again, Paul Meyer says in *Fragments d'une Vie de S. Thomas de Cantorbéry*, p. xxxi : ' Il n'existe pas, selon moi, de règle générale s'appliquant à la versification des poètes français d'Angleterre.' In many other places P. Meyer repeats this view, e. g. in his review of my pamphlet *Sur la Versification Anglo-Normande*, in *Ro.* xv. 145. Tobler expresses the same opinion in his treatise *Vom franz. Versbau*, p. 11, n. 2. The present writer has on many occasions expressed the same opinion, first in the above-quoted pamphlet, later in his editions of Anglo-Norman texts, as well as in several articles in the *Jahresb. rom. Ph.* and in the *Literaturbl. für germanische und romanische Philologie*.

There are, nevertheless, philologists that hold another opinion. Atkinson, ten Brink, Suchier, Foerster, Koch, Gnerlich, Stimming, Baker, Macaulay, and others, suppose that the Anglo-Norman poets combined certain features of the English metrical system, especially English rhythm, with the French system, and that they applied very intricate rules of caesura. The untenableness of this theory has been sufficiently demonstrated by P. Meyer (*Athenaeum*, June 24, 1876, *Ro.* xv. 147), Koschwitz (*Z. f. rom. Ph.* ii. 388), as well as in my pamphlet *Sur la Versification Anglo-Normande* ; cf. also Tobler, loc. cit. Here we will confine ourselves to the following observations. The Anglo-Norman poets were in general, even if they belonged to the clergy, people of little learning, and what they possessed least of all was system and theory. Most of them did not know English or knew it only imperfectly, and at the same time they found no little difficulty, as they themselves admit, in handling the French language and French versification. How was it possible for them to construct out of two metrical systems they hardly knew a new and very complicated system ? And if they had done so they would certainly have boasted of it, instead of confessing their incapacity in metrical matters. A remarkable fact seems to confirm this view. The author of a *Life of Pope Clement* (No. 110) at the beginning of his work writes in very bad verse, but continues later in good metre. This no doubt means that he has learnt versification in the course of writing his long poem of 15,000 lines. Furthermore, it may be said that the Anglo-Norman incorrectness in respect of the number of syllables has a parallel in the not infrequent inexactness of the stanzas and the couplets, facts which betray a generally weak metrical sense.

There is, however, an exception to be noticed in John Gower's versification. But it is to be observed that he was a learned man, who had spent considerable time in Paris, and was, as an English poet, familiar with English versification. For him it was possible to combine adherence to English rhythm with the French syllabic system. For the details of Gower's verse see Macaulay's Introduction, pp. xv, xliv, lxxiii, lxxxiv.

A peculiarity in the counting of the syllables is to be found in *St. Brendan* and some other texts. It consists in counting the post-tonic *e* in the rhyme-word as the eighth syllable, whereas this *e* is an extra syllable in French verse (cf. my *Étude,* p. 44, *Purg. de S. Patrice,* p. 9, and Birkenhoff, *Über Metr. u. Reim der altfranz. Brandanlegende*). This peculiarity is a feature of Nos. 44, 45, 104. In Nos. 44, 45, however, the line is hexasyllabic, and the post-tonic *e* in the rhyme is counted as the sixth syllable. To a French ear this makes an incomprehensible line, as appears from the alterations in the French ms. of *Brendan* (*388*).

In some poems it would seem that the use of this kind of octosyllabic feminine line has led the author often to shorten his octosyllabics to heptasyllabics. Such is the case in Nos. 80, 101, 212. On the versification of No. 101, *Vie de Thomas de Cantorbéry,* Paul Meyer remarks: ' Nous caractériserons donc la versification de l'auteur inconnu de la vie de saint Thomas en disant que dans ce poème les vers de huit et de sept syllabes sont admis indistinctement. Une telle irrégularité serait incroyable de la part d'un poète proprement français. . . . Il n'est pas contestable que cet auteur avait l'oreille peu faite à la cadence des vers français.' The probable explanation of such peculiarities is that given above, the uncertainty in counting the post-tonic *e*. A conscious or intentional mixture of octosyllabic and heptasyllabic lines often occurs in modern French poetry ; it was rare in early times. P. Meyer has noticed one example of it, a poem of Guillaume de Deguille-ville (*Vie de S. Thomas de Cantorbéry*, p. xxxiv).

Another attempt to account for the metrical irregularity of Anglo-Norman poems by attributing it to the negligence or ignorance of the copyists was made by Hermann Rose in an article in *Rom. Stud.* v. 301. I have attempted to refute this theory in my pamphlet *Sur la Versification Anglo-Normande*, p. 24. See also Tobler's remarks, *Vom franz. Versbau*, p. 11, n. 2.

Finally, it is to be observed that the unity of the metre is not infrequently broken in the course of the same poem. This is a phenomenon that occurs also in continental poems, though rarely; cf. Tobler, op. cit., p. 10. We find it in the following poems: No. 115, where a speech in lines of fourteen syllables is inserted among alexandrines; No. 120, where 200 lines, approximatively octosyllabic, are followed by longer lines extending to thirteen syllables; No. 132, which presents the same case; No. 228, where after a short introduction in octosyllabics there follows a poem in hepta-syllabics; No. 302, which resembles 132; No. 212, eight and ten syllables.

In the *Mystère d'Adam* the change of metre is evidently intentional. Professor Studer says of this change: ' In rapid dialogues, in the glib speech of Satan, in the angry words of God, and Adam's rage at realizing his lost estate, he gives preference to octosyllabic verse, reserving the longer metre for the solemn installation of man in Paradise, the sorrow of Eve after the Fall, and the lament of Adam ' (p. lii).

The change of metre in Philipe's *Bestiaire* in the editions is apparent only. In reality Philipe begins a new poem where this change is introduced; cf. the remark on No. 67. In Fantosme's *Chronicle* there is also a passage of 120 lines (646–765) in a different metre from the preceding and the following lines. Those 120 lines are doubtless an intercalation.

The very rare metre of 16 syllables is not quite unknown in Anglo-Norman poetry; see *Ro.* xv. 309, 321, xxxii. 110, and Nos. 95, 173, 189.

F 2

§ 2. Hiatus, Elision, Enclisis

Since the French rules of hiatus and elision depend on the vocal value of the post-tonic *e*, their application is of little force where this value is uncertain. Therefore it is only in the older. and (from a French point of view) correct, poems that the French system of hiatus and elision can be said to be observed. It may be, however, that Anglo-Norman poets extended the use of hiatus. Thus they may have regarded as a full octosyllabic the following line of Gaimar's *Chronicle* (1006):

> Si firent rei de Edelfriz,

with hiatus before a proper name. Further, they might have read, as the copyists wrote, *de els*, *de autre*, *le emperur*, *se est*, *me oez*, &c. with hiatus. Cf. my *Stud. i den franska Romanen om Horn*, ii, p. 21, and the literature quoted there. But these are mere speculations.

Enclisis is regularly applied in the oldest texts; cf. Walberg, *Le Bestiaire de Philipe de Thaun*, p. xl, and the above-cited *Stud. in Horn*, ii, p. 1. In *Horn* enclisis abounds. Soon afterwards it becomes more and more rare, as it does on the Continent (cf. Rydberg, *Geschichte des franz. E*, p. 453, and *passim*). The manuscripts very often omit it where the author evidently intended it. Cf. Walberg, loc. cit.

§ 3. Caesura

French verses of ten, twelve, or more syllables generally have a pause or caesura in the interior of the verse. For the rules of the caesura reference may be made to any manual of metrics, e. g. those of Tobler or Kastner. It is probable that the octosyllabic line never has had a caesura, as it has not in modern times; cf. Tobler, p. 109. In Anglo-Norman literature there is one curious exception, viz. in *St. Brendan* (No. 10). There the octosyllabic lines are very regularly divided into two halves; cf. *Sur la Versif. Anglo-N.*, p. 53. In the older Anglo-Norman literature, before French versification in general came to be neglected, poems in decasyllabic or longer lines were rare. Thus few examples of correct cæsura occur. Examples are, however, to be found in Nos. 9, 22, 25, 27, and perhaps in No. 18 (cf. Spencer, p. 12).

It is possible that the Anglo-Norman poets had a particular kind of caesura, which I have called ' Anglo-Norman caesura' in *Stud. i den franska Rom. om Horn*, i, p. 19 (cf. Suchier in *Gesch. der franz. Liter.*, p. 113, Gnerlich, p. 25). This caesura falls after a post-tonic *e* in the sixth syllable, e. g. *Horn*, 1762:

> E reis Hunlaf l'eime . cum l'oust engendré.

It recurs so often in *Horn* that it seems to have been intentional. Cf. *Jahresb. rom. Ph.* VII. i. 197. It may have been applied in other poems also, but as they are more irregular this caesura may be in this case accidental.

To propose numerous special rules for the caesura is tantamount to abolishing it altogether. It is improbable that the Anglo-Norman poets had such an intricate theory of caesura as is assumed by Stimming in his edition of *Boeve*, or Baker in his edition of *Richard*. And how, we may ask, would it be possible to make the lines of (e. g.) Nos. 8, 12, 37 correct in respect of the caesura?

§ 4. Couplets, Enjambement, Stanza

P. Meyer has shown (*Ro.* xxiii. 1) that in Old French literature hexasyllabic and octosyllabic lines were grouped in couplets. This is also the case in Anglo-Norman literature, though examples of breach of the couplet are as early as Philipe de Thaun's poems (cf. Walberg's ed. of the *Bestiaire*, p. xxi) and Gaimar's *Chronicle* (examples in Meyer's article). But on the whole *enjambement* is rare in Anglo-Norman poetry. The most striking examples are those afforded by the *Vie S. Edmund* of Denis Piramus (No. 14) and a *Life of Edward the Confessor* (No. 125). In the former poem we find:

> Kant la tere e le païs feu
> Si longement sanz chief segnur (1612);
>
> Que son groin aveit apuié
> Sur le frunt, mais la face aperte
> Out, e la buche descoverte (2756);

> Ke la cité par force prendre
> Voelent, s'il ne se voelent rendre
> A els, &c. (3397).

In the latter :

> Of autres enseignes ke ai
> Dit, la verité ben sai (2236);
>
> Kar Seint Pere, ki est vicaire
> Deu, ca co dist suvent repaire (2240);
>
> Ore venge dunc avant, de part
> Deu, ki bone garaisun
> L'en doint par ma beneicun (2985).

The stanza is in general artless, mostly isometric, and with a plain disposition of the rhyme. A comparatively frequent, non-monorhyme stanza is the following, isometric or heterometric: *aabaab*, or *aabccb*. It occurs often in Bozon's poems.

More complicated stanzas are represented by the following poems: No. 52, *aaaabbbaba*; No. 58, *8a8a8a8a4b10b*; No. 93, *aabaabbbabba*; No. 240, *aabbbccc*; No. 246, *ababccbddb*; No. 280, *abababab2c14c*. There are stanzas of eighteen lines, as in Nos. 228, 245 (with refrain), of twenty-four lines, as in two of the poems in No. 228. Cf. Naetebus, *Die ... Stro- phenformen des Altfranz.* (1901). In two instances still more artistic stanzas, typical of the Provençal-French lyric poetry, are imitated, viz. in No. 85, *ababccddecec* with an interior rhyme (*dd*); and in No. 237, a tenzon, where the first three stanzas have the same rhyme, and the two follow- ing stanzas the same rhyme, the form of the stanza being *aabaabbbabba*.

An example of ballade is afforded by Gower (No. 360).

A refrain is found in Nos. 245, 271, and in 84, where it is in Latin.

In one poem the stanzas are linked together by *rimes couées* (No. 6).

In some poems by Bozon the stanzas are linked by *enjambement*; e. g. in the *Plainte d'Amour* (No. 357):

> St. cxxi def: Ki riches sunt e unt a doner
>   E lur parenz pount avancer
>   Tant solement
> St. cxxii a : Serrunt amez e honurez.

St. clviii ef: Or ren ne pensent de autre garde
For de waster
St. clix a: Boys e gardins e pasture.

In the *Parabole du demi-ami* (No. 365):
St. 11 ef: S'il ne sache acunte rendre,
Tant est iree,
St. 12 a: De chescun dener e maille.

See *Ro.* xxxv. 48 (P. Meyer).

Very often the stanzas are unequal in length—a further evidence of the lack of a sense of French versification so characteristic of Anglo-Norman poets. Stanzas varying in length in the same poem are to be found in the following: Nos. 8, 44, 46, 74, 87, 146, 177, 239, 241, 265, 284, 358, 401. In No. 271 the stanzas are irregular in respect of the rhyme.

There are to be found also laisses after the model of the French *chansons de geste*, e. g. in Nos. 118, 140, 213, 354.

Examples of acrostics are afforded by Simund de Freine in his two poems Nos. 16, 55.

§ 5. Rhyme

In the earliest poems the rhymes are generally correct from an Anglo-Norman (or Norman) point of view. Thus we ought to consider as correct the rhymes *segur : seingnor*, Angier (cf. Pope, p. 20), *maur : seur* in a laisse on *-or* in *S. Alban* (laisse xvii), &c., and later, *moster : pere* (*Ro.* iv. 376), &c.; cf. *Sur la Versification Anglo-N.*, p. 65. But there are also poets who are very negligent in their rhymes, as, for instance, the author of the *Riote* (No. 268), *potters : demaundez*, l. 135, *volenters : priez*, l. 147, *vyle : dire*, l. 223, &c. No. 271 has not only irregular but very defective rhymes. No. 165 ought to be considered as lacking rhymes, though there are not a few lines with similar endings. No. 147 passes from verse to prose.

On the other hand there are even examples of exquisite rhymes. Professor Freymond in his study of the rich and the leonine rhyme (*Z. f. rom. Ph.* vi. 1) has quoted some Anglo-Norman texts where such rhymes occur, as *St.*

Brendan (No. 10), in which these rhymes are in the proportion of 27%; *Lumière as lais* (No. 157), 23%, the *Housse partie* (No. 216), 21%, the *Computus* of Philipe (No. 64), 19%; his *Bestiaire* (No. 65), 18%, &c.

A peculiarity of Anglo-Norman rhyming is that, instead of the two rhymes of the couplet, there are often three, four, or more rhymes. P. Meyer has often called attention to this peculiarity, e. g. *Ro.* xv. 272, 297, xxiii. 8, 28; *S. Thomas de Cantorbéry*, p. xxxv; *Not. et Extr.* XXXII. ii. 78. It occurs early and in some of the most correct poems, as in the *Mystère d'Adam* (cf. Studer, p. lii) and in *La Folie Tristan*, 341; in the first of the poems quoted under No. 228; and in less accurate poems such as those quoted by P. Meyer, loc. cit. In one of these poems, composed in couplets, there is a passage of thirty-five lines having the same rhyme. In the *Riote* (No. 268) there are five rhymes, ll. 251 and 259, three rhymes, ll. 270 ff.

VIII.   LIST OF MANUSCRIPTS

Title of MS.	Date (*Century*).	Contents.	No.
LONDON		(nos. of works in pp. 41. ff.)	
BRITISH MUSEUM			
Roy. 1 C iii	XV	352	1
2 D xiii	early XIV	78	2
4 C xi	XIII	20 Note	3
8 E xvii	early XIV	96, 113, 155, 259, 265, 291	4
8 F ix	XIV	212	5
11 B iii	XIII–XIV	93, 184, 190	6
12 C xii	middle XIV	35, 85, 156, 214, 284, 384	7
12 D xi	early XIV	385	8
12 F xiii	early XIII	68	9
13 A iv	XIII–XIV	386	10
13 A xviii	XIV	367	11
13 A xxi	2nd half XIII	61, 62	12
15 D ii	early XIV	76, 157	13
16 E ii	XV	184, 304	14
16 E viii	XIII	84, 239, 240	15
16 E ix	XIII	157	16
19 B xv	early XIV	76	17
19 C v	early XIII	7	18
19 C ix	1st half XV	378h	19

Title of MS.	*Date (Century).*	*Contents.*	*No.*
BRITISH MUSEUM (*continued*):			
Roy. 20 A ii	XIV	377	20
20 A iii	2nd half XIV	378h	21
20 A xi	XIV	377, 393	22
20 A xviii	XIV	378i	23
20 B v	late XIV	250	24
20 B xiv	XIII–XIV	25, 55, 97, 124, 146-7, 153, 154, 210, 254	25
20 C vi	XIV	298	26
App. 85	XV	378h	27
Cott. Jul. A i	XIV	378d	28
A v	XIV	96, 300, 355, 377	29
D v	XIV	376	30
D vii	XIII	246, 324	31
Tib. A vi	XIV	378a	32
Cal. A ix	1st half XIII	20, 21, 56, 298	33
A xviii	XIV	233, 244, 301	34
Claud. D iii	middle XIII	207	35
Nero A v	2nd half XII	64, 65, 67	36
C iv	early XIII	1 ·	37
D ii	XIV	376	38
D vi	late XIV	299	39
Vitell. A x	late XIII	295	40
C viii	XIV	361	41
D iii	middle XIII	8	42
Vesp. A vi	XIV	386	43
A vii	early XIV	17, 32	44
B x	late XII	10	45
B xiv	late XIII	19	46
D iv	XIV	19	47
Titus D xx	late XIII	321	48
Domit. A iv	XIII	102	49
A x	XIV	378c	50
A xi	early XIV	14, 75, 121, 134, 154	51
A xviii	XIV	299	52
Cleop. A vi	XIV	380	53
A xii	2nd half XIII	99, 295	54
B ix	2nd half XIII	367	54a
D iii	XV	378h	55
D vii	XIV–XV	378c	56
D ix	XIV	378d	57
Harley 200	XV	378e	58
209	early XIV	281, 287	59
273	1st half XIV	1, 90, 104, 158, 183, 198, 202, 320, 328, 357	60
337	early XIV	158	61
490	XIV	386	62
505	early XIV	188	63

Title of MS.	Date (Century).	Contents.	No.
BRITISH MUSEUM (continued):			
Harley 527	late XIII	31, 54	64
636	XIV	376	65
645		343	66
740	XIV	386	67
746	late XIII	284, 300	68
902	early XVII	375	69
912	middle XIV	15	70
913	XIV	296	71
957	XIV	257, 265	72
978	2nd half XIII	266, 286, 325	73
1121	XIV	153, 156	74
1348	XIII	294	75
1770	XIV	1	76
1801	XIII	289	77
2253	early XIV	9, 43, 51, 60, 82, 87, 111, 112, 148, 182, 184, 217, 218, 219, 231, 235, 242, 243, 245, 256, 268, 280, 282, 285, 286, 366, 371	78
3775	middle XIV	19, 193, 212, 353	79
3988	XV	241, 389, 391	80
4070	early XIII	6	81
4388	early XIII	4, 22, 44, 54	82
4390	XIII	157	83
4657	XIV	46, 158, 201, 257	84
4733	XIII	61	85
4971	XIV	23, 158, 387, 391	86
5102	1st half XIII	1	87
6359	middle XIV	378d	88
Lansdowne 383	XIII	106	89
397	XIV	187, 385	90
1117	XIII	294	91
Arundel 57	middle XIV	300	92
220	early XIV	297, 307, 386	93
230	late XII	1, 6, 64	94
248	XIV	199, 200	95
288	XIV	154, 184, 190, 361	96
292	late XIII	23, 45, 289	97
507	late XIV	257, 265	98
Sloane 513	XIV	386	99
809	XIV	386	100
1580	early XIII	64	101
1611	XIII	120, 177	102
1986	XIV	328	102a
Stowe 948	early XIV	198	103
Addit. 5762	XIV	328	104
6159	XIV	329	105
10622	XV	378i	106

Title of MS.	*Date (Century).*	*Contents.*	*No*
BRITISH MUSEUM (*continued*):			
Addit. 17716	XV	389, 391, 402	107
18462a	early XV	378d, 378h	108
18462b	early XV	378d	109
18633	middle XIV	78	110
22283	XIII	45, 265	111
26773	middle XIII	71	112
35092	middle XIV	378a	113
35113	XIV	378c	114
38662	middle XIII	212	115
38664	about 1240	13, 117	116
(*olim* Edwardes)			
Egerton 612	XII–XIII	13	117
613	XIII	198, 204, 232, 271	118
1066	2nd half XIII	130	119
2515	1st half XIV	32, 33	120
2710	2nd half XIII	9, 22, 100	121
COLLEGE OF ARMS			
27	XIV	212	122
Arundel xiv	1st half XIV	39, 61, 252, 298, 377	123
xxxi	XIV	378d	124
lxi	XIV	377	125
RECORD OFFICE			
Exchequer 24	XIII	298	126
INNER TEMPLE			
Dir. 8/9 Shelf 1			
No. 511, 19		378d	127
LINCOLN'S INN			
88	XV	378h	128
GRAY'S INN			
12	middle XIV	368	129
GRESHAM COLL.			
C 56		379	130
LAMBETH PALACE			
371		45	131
403	about 1300	333	132
504		378d	133
522	1st half XIV (cf. 79)	74, 79, 83, 88, 90–92, 153, 159, 161, 162, 164, 166, 168, 170, 177, 178, 181, 184, 208	134
596	late XIII	292	135
THE TOWER	XIV	387	136
Guildhall		343	137
OXFORD			
BODLEIAN LIBRARY			
Ashmole 1285	2nd half XIII	225	138
1470		319	139

Title of MS.	Date (Century).	Contents.	No.
BODLEIAN LIBRARY (continued):			
Ashmole 1804	early XV	378h	140
Bodley 9	XIV	187, 247, 390	141
57	2nd half XIII	88, 90, 173, 184, 185, 319, 320	142
82	1st half XIV	365	143
90	2nd half XIII	167	144
399	XIII	153, 157, 303	145
425	late XIV	247, 265, 291	146
761	2nd half XIV	265, 314, 319, 383	147
Digby 20	late XIII	167	148
34	early XIII	107	149
53	early XIII	48, 49	150
86	late XIII	40, 54, 59, 88, 94, 159, 166, 168, 184, 195, 266, 269, 270, 274, 279, 289, 307, 311, 319	151
103	XIV	86	152
172		322	153
204	XIV	328	154
Douce 88	late XIII	326	155
98	XIV	328	156
115	XIII	298	157
119	XV	379	158
120	XIV	377	159
128	XV	378e	160
132	middle XIII	31, 153	161
137	XIII	159, 234, 246	162
210	late XIII	25, 51, 55, 57, 145, 156, 190, 247, 249, 253, 287, 302	163
282	XIII	143	164
320	1st half XII	1, 26	165
381	XIII	17	166
d. 6	XIII–XIV	30, 34, 180, 255	167
Fairfax 24	early XIV	237, 290, 377	168
Graves 51	middle XIV	95	169
Hatton 99	XIV	153, 158	170
James 19	XIV	379	171
Laud Misc. 79	late XIII	167	172
471	XIV	139, 153	173
Rawl. B 178	XIV	379	174
C 46		167	175
C 504	XIII	290	176
C 641	XII–XIII	50	177
D 329	XIV	298, 378d	178
D 913 (= Misc. 1370)	XIII	10, 24, 32, 33, 212	179
Poetry 241	1st half XIV	98, 132, 154, 155, 156	180

Title of MS.	Date (Century).	Contents.	No.
BODLEIAN LIBRARY (*continued*) :			
(Rawl. Misc. 473		265, 290, 302, 357	
in *Z. f. fr. S.*			
u. L. xiv. 128)			
Selden supra 38	XIV	80	181
74	XIV	47, 149, 156, 171, 196, 248, 257, 265, 298, 361, 386	182
Tanner 195	XIV	298	183
Vernon	XIII	45, 265	184
Wood	XIV	378c	185
ALL SOULS COLL.			
39	XIV	374, 377	186
182	XIV	386, 388, 389, 391, 400	187
CORP. CHR. COLL.			
36	late XIII	9, 144, 156	188
59	XIII	305	189
78	early XIV	378f	190
135	XIII	275, 319	191
154	XIII	243	192
182	XIII	261	193
232	early XIV	20 Note, 153	194
293	XIV	378d	195
JESUS COLL. 29	middle XIII	20, 21, 56	196
ST. JOHN'S COLL.			
75	early XIV	167, 168	197
178	XIII	44, 306, 319, 321, 322	198
183	XIV	130	199
190	XIII	144	200
204	XIV	303	201
MAGDALEN COLL.			
40	XII	197	202
45	XIV	379	203
188	early XV	387	204
221	XV	319	205
MERTON COLL.			
249	XIII	65	206
321	XIV	329	207
ORIEL COLL.			
XLVI	XIV	381	208
TRINITY COLL.			
7	XV	184, 264	209
82	late XIII	206	210
UNIVERSITY COLL.			
LXXII	late XIII	75NB	211
[Robartes	middle XIII	37	212]
CAMBRIDGE			
UNIVERSITY LIBRARY			
Dd 10. 31	late XIII	228, 302	213

Title of MS.	Date (Century).	Contents.	No.
UNIVERSITY LIBRARY (continued):			
Dd 12. 23	early XV	389, 402	214
15. 12	late XIII	30	215
Ee 1. 1	late XIII	329, 332	216
1. 20	XIV	158, 378g	217
3. 59	middle XIII	125	218
4. 20	about 1340	327, 387, 391	219
6. 11	2nd half XIII	18, 105	220
6. 16	XIV	184, 195, 205	221
6. 30	XIII	98	222
Ff 6. 13		310, 311	223
6. 15	2nd half XIV	176	224
6. 17	late XIII	31	225
Gg 1. 1	early XIV	71, 80, 89, 95, 97, 157, 158, 168, 173, 180, 184, 185, 203, 247, 257, 273, 278, 300, 303, 305, 357, 358, 377, 378b, 386	226
1. 15	XIV	184, 185, 378d	227
4. 32	2nd half XIV	173	228
6. 28	1st half XIV	291, 302	229
Hh 3. 11		329	230
Ii 6. 17	late XV	403	231
Jj 6. 8	XV	378h	232
Kk 4. 20	XIV	289	233
Mm 1. 33	XIV	378c	234
6. 4	XIV	158	235
6. 15	XIV	20 Note	236
Addit. 3035	late XIV	369	237
3303	about 1300	251	238
4164	about 1200	64	239
CAIUS COLL.			
11	middle XIV	229	240
54	1st half XIV	238	241
CLARE COLL.			
3. 6 (with Kk 3. 10, Kk 3. 13)		1, 19, 25	242
CORP. CHR. COLL.			
20	1st half XIV	78, 133	243
50	middle XIII	35, 212, 220, 289, 374	244
53	XIV	298	245
66	XIV	81, 116	246
98	about 1470	298	247
133	XIV	308, 382	248
150	XIV	319	249
278	early XIV	1	250
301	XIV	319	251
335	XV	319	252

List of Manuscripts

Title of MS.	Date (Century).	Contents.	No.
CORP. CHR. COLL. (continued):			
383	XIII	320	253
388	XIV	319	254
405	2nd half XIII	17, 23, 44, 88, 154, 184, 300	255
450	XIV	226, 227, 257, 258, 267, 386	256
462	XIII	164	257
EM. COLL. I. 4. 4	late XIII	165	258
GONV. AND CAIUS COLL.			
424	middle XIV	312	259
435	1st half XIII	12, 17, 58	260
JESUS COLL.			
Q. D. 2	about 1200	66	261
Q. G. 10	XIV	382	262
ST. JOHN'S COLL.			
D. 4	XIII–XIV	319	263
E. 9	XIII	235, 306	264
E. 26	XV	184	265
F. 1	XIII	235	266
F. 30	2nd half XIII	157, 158	267
G. 5	XV	278	268
I. 11	late XIII ?	302	269
256	XIV	172	270
MAGDALEN COLL.			
1803	middle XIV	78	271
PEMBROKE COLL.			
111	XIII	68	272
112	XII–XIII	186	273
258	XIII, XIV	20 Note	274
TRINITY COLL.			
B. 1. 45	XIII	141	275
B. 14. 39	XIII	71, 73, 150, 151, 165, 192, 194, 263	276
B. 14. 40	about 1415	247, 392, 401, 402	277
B. 15. 36		320	278
O. 1. 17	XIV	156, 180, 247, 357	279
O. 1. 20	XIII	168, 313, 314, 315, 319	280
O. 2. 5	XIV	308, 319	281
O. 2. 14	1st half XIII	25, 143	282
O. 2. 21	XIV	386	283
O. 2. 29	XIII	142, 173	284
O. 2. 45	XIII	168, 189, 268, 319, 320	285
O. 3. 45	early XIV	349	286
O. 4. 32	XIV	293, 379	287
O. 5. 32	early XV	90, 306, 308	288
O. 7. 9	XIII	321	289
O. 7. 37	XIV	320	290
O. 8. 27	XIII–XIV	319	291

Title of MS.	Date (Century).	Contents.	No.
TRINITY COLL. (*continued*) :			
O. 2. 29	XIV–XVI	320	292
C. 9. 34	late XIII	37	293
R. 3. 46	middle XIII	109, 110	294
R. 4. 26	XIV	378a	295
R. 7. 14	1st half XIV	378d	296
R. 7. 23	XIV	306, 378	297
R. 14. 7	about 1300	170, 172, 174, 298, 318, 373	298
R. 15. 2	about 1240	76	299
R. 17. 1	about 1160	2	300
Addit. 4407, 4470	XIII	31	301
FITZWILLIAM MUS.			
123	about 1300	78, 153	302
CHELTENHAM (formerly *PHILLIPPS*)			
3713	late XIII	39, 41, 53	303
4156	2nd half XIII	9, 54, 70, 103, 304, 307	304
8113	XIII	19	305
8188		386, 389	306
8336	1st half XIV	52, 55, 86, 88, 96, 152, 160, 163, 175, 177, 184, 185, 211, 236, 260, 282, 288, 291, 310, 312, 355, 356, 357, 359, 361, 362, 363, 364, 368, 386	307
8345	XIV	38, 212	308
25970	middle XIV	42, 216, 272, 354, 393	309
DURHAM CATHEDRAL			
A ii. 11	about 1200	7	310
C iv. 27	early XIII	61, 69	311
C iv. 27 B	XIV	37	312
LINCOLN CATHEDRAL			
A 4	late XIII	61, 62, 69	313
C 33	about 1250	64	314
WORCESTER CATHEDRAL			
35	XIII	304	315
YORK CATHEDRAL			
16. I. 7	XIII	212	316
16. K. 7	XIV	158	317
16. K. 12	2nd half XIII	10	318
16. K. 13	XIII	118, 128, 135, 158	319
16. K. 14	2nd half XIII	71	320
16. N. 3	1267	157	321
HEREFORD CATHEDRAL			
P. III, 3		262	322
DULWICH			
Alleyne Coll.			
22	XIII	13	323
Oscott Coll.		6	324

Title of MS.	Date (Century).	Contents.	No.
SOUTHAMPTON			
BOROUGH AR-CHIVES	XIV–XV	395	325
EVERINGHAM PARK	XIV	158	326
CANTERBURY Roy. J. & P.	XIV	329	327
LONGLEAT (Marquess of Bath)	XIV	68, 262, 359a	327a
MARSKE HALL	2nd half XIII	212	328
TRENTHAM HALL	early XV	360	329
WELBECK I C I	early XIV	11, 107, 122, 123, 134, 137, 138	330
DUKE OF NOR-FOLK	XIV	158	331
HOLKHAM (Nor-folk)	about 1230	331	332
WOLLATON HALL	XIII	71, 158	333
EDINBURGH ADVOCATES	early XIV	317, 319 (two mss.)	334
LIBRARY	early XIV	372	334a
GLASGOW HUNTERIAN MUSEUM			
Q. 9. 13	XIII	303	335
R. 6. 12		307	336
R. 7. 14	middle XIII	323	337
DUBLIN TRINITY COLL.			
B. 5. 1	XIII	157	338
C. 4. 2 (312)	XIV	140, 179, 184	339
D. 4. 18	XIII	129, 154, 184, 209	340
E. 1. 40	XIII	115	341
500	XIV	378d	342
501	XIV	378h	343
MUNICIPAL AR-CHIVES		345	344
SNEYD (lost)		30	345
PARIS BIBL. NATIONALE			
fonds fr. 1	XIV	352	346
898	XIV	9	347
902	2nd half XIII	9, 16, 19, 28, 153, 154, 223	348
1669	XIII	212	349
1768	XIV	76	350

Title of MS.	Date (Century).	Contents.	No.
BIBL. NATIONALE (*continued*) :			
fonds fr. 2169	XIV	33	351
2198	XV	104	352
6447	about 1275	5	353
7011	XIV	329	354
9562	2nd half XIV	352	355
12154	XIV	377	356
12155	2nd half XV	378h	357
12156	2nd half XV	378d	358
13342	XIV	156	359
13505	XIII	131	360
14640	about 1300	378a	361
14959	XIV	158	362
19152	XIII	54	363
19525	2nd half XIII	17, 22, 25, 100, 119, 143, 168	364
20047	XIII	36	365
23112	middle XIII	11	366
24364	about 1300	37	367
24766	1214	108	368
24862	middle XIII	72, 111, 112, 113, 114	369
25407	XIII	25, 45, 250	370
Nouv. acq. 1104	late XIII	41	371
1404	2nd half XIII	5	372
4267	1337	378a	373
4503	middle XII	10, 11	374
4532	XIV	213, 298	375
5237	XIV	9	376
7517	late XIII	54	377
10061	XIV	157	378
(Piot) 11198	early XIV	71	379
fonds lat. 217	XVI	321	380
768	late XII	1	381
770	XV	307	382
873	early XIII	68	383
1315	XII	185	384
7679	XV	321	385
8846	early XIII	2	386
Nouv. acq. 1670	late XII	1	387
BIBL. DE L'ARSENAL			
3516	2nd half XIII	10	388
5211	middle XIII	5	389
BIBL. MAZARINE			
54	about 1170	5	390
1860	XV	378h	391
BIBL. GENEVIEVE			
935	2nd half XV	378h	392
BIBL. DIDOT	2nd half XIII	213	393
CAMBRAI 867 (875) XIII		321	393a

Title of MS.	Date (Century).	Contents.	No.
CHANTILLY			
Musée Condé			
724	XIV	5	394
COURTRAI	1st half XIII	101	395
PUY-DE-DÔME			
Archives	late XIII	222	396
ROUEN			
Bibl. Munic.			
O. 35 (1425)	XIII	54	397
STRASSBURG	XIII	30	lost
TOULOUSE			
Bibl. Munic. 815	middle XIV	78, 133	398
TOURS			
Bibl. Munic.			
237	middle XIII	20 Note	399
927	late XII	27	400
948	middle XIV	103	401
BRUGES 536	XIII	321	402
BRUSSELS			
Bibl. Royale			
B 282	XIII	157, 180	403
9903	XIV	376	403a
FLORENCE			
Laurentiana			
Conventi Sop-			
pressi 99	early XIII	15	404
Plut. xviii, dextr.			
No. 7	XIII	257	405
Plut. xli	XIII	60	406
ROME			
Vatican,			
Reg. 489	XIII	126	407
1659	late XIV	56, 276, 302	408
not numbered		298, 373	409
TURIN			
Private	1st half XIII	30	410
GÖTTINGEN			
Bibl. No. 184	1st half XIII	29	411
HAMBURG			
Municipal			
Library	XIV	169	412
KARLSRUHE			
Grand Duke's			
Library	2nd half XIV	35	413
MUNICH			
Municipal Li-			
brary Cod.			
Gall. 7	XII-XIII	61	414

Title of MS.	Date (Century).	Contents.	No.
TRIER			
Jesuit Coll. No. 2			
& 5 (*Ro.* xvi.			
177)	XIII–XIV	9, 136	415
WOLFFENBÜTTEL			
Cod. Aug.			
No. 87. 4	late XIII	212	416
COPENHAGEN			
Roy. Library			
Gamle Kungl.			
Saml. 3466	XIII	65	417
Thott 89	middle XIV	78	418
AMERICA			
Fox	middle XIV	77	419

BIBLIOGRAPHY

PART I

CHAPTER I

Adams, G. B., *The History of England from the Norman Conquest to the death of John*, in *The Political History of England* (vol. ii, 1905).

Behrens, D., *Französische Elemente im Englischen*, in *Grundriss der germanischen Philologie*.

Brandin, L., *Anglo-Norman*, in *Encyclopaedia Britannica*, 11th ed.

Clover, B., *French Language in England from the Eleventh to the Fourteenth Century*. 1888.

Craik, G. L., *A compendious History of English Literature and of the English Language from the Norman Conquest*, 1st ed. 1861.

Davis, H. W. C., *Regesta Regum Anglo-Normannorum*, vol. i, 1066–1100. 1913.

Déprez, Eugène, *Études de diplomatique anglaise*. 1908.

Earle, John, *The Philology of the English Tongue*, 5th ed. 1892.

Emerson, O. F., *The History of the English Language*. 1894.

—— *English or French in the time of Edward III?* in *Romanic Review*, 1916, vol. vii. 127.

Fiedler, F., and Kölbing, E., *Wissenschaftliche Grammatik der englischen Sprache*, 2nd ed. 1877.

Freeman, E. A., *History of the Norman Conquest*, 6 vols. 1867–79 (especially vol. v).

Hill, Geoffry, *Some Consequences of the Norman Conquest*. 1904.

Jusserand, J. J., *Histoire littéraire du peuple anglais*, 2nd ed. 1907.

Lounsbury, T. R., *History of the English Language*. 1879 (pp. 59 ff.).

Low, W. H., *The English Language: its History and Structure*, 1st ed. 1892. Several new editions.

Maitland, F. W., *Year Books of Edward II*. Introd. 1903.

Meyer, Paul, *Les Contes moralisés de Nicole Bozon*. Introd., ch. iii. 1889.

Paris, G., *L'Esprit normand en Angleterre*, in *La Poésie du moyen âge*, 2ᵐᵉ série. 1895.

Pollock, F. and Maitland, F. W., *The History of English Law*, 2nd vol., 2nd ed. 1898 (vol. i, p. 79 seq.).

Scheibner, O., *Über die Herrschaft der französischen Sprache in England*. 1880.

Studer, Paul, *The Study of Anglo-Norman*. 1920.

Tanquerey, F. J., *L'Évolution du verbe en anglo-français*. 1915.—Idem, *Recueil de Lettres anglo-françaises (1265–1399)*. 1916.

Thommerel, J. P., *Recherches sur la fusion du franconormand et de l'anglosaxon*. 1841.

Tout, T. F., *The History of England from the accession of Henry III to the death of Edward III*, in *The Political History of England*, vol. iii. 1905.

Vising, J., *Franska Språket i England*, i–iii. 1900–2.

Watkin, Morgan, *The French Linguistic Influence in Mediaeval Wales,* Trans. Hon. Soc. of Cymmrodorion, Sess. 1918–19, pp. 146–222 ; *The French Literary Influence in Mediaeval Wales,* ibid., Sess. 1919–20, pp. 1–81.

CHAPTER II

Behrens, D., *Beiträge zur Geschichte der franz. Sprache in England.* 1886.
Brink, B. ten, *Chaucers Sprache und Verskunst,* 1st ed. 1884.
Busch, E., *Laut- und Formenlehre der anglonorm. Sprache des vierzehnten Jahrhunderts.* 1887.
Menger, L. E., *The Anglo-Norman Dialect.* 1904.
Pope, Mildred K., *Étude sur la langue de Frère Angier.* 1904.
Schwan-Behrens, *Grammaire de l'ancien français.* 1913.
Stimming, A., *Der anglonormannische Boeve de Haumtone.* 1899.
Suchier, H., *Les Voyelles toniques du vieux français.* 1906.
—— *Über die Matthäus Paris zugeschriebene Vie de saint Auban.* 1876.
Tanneberger, A., *Sprachliche Untersuchung der franz. Werke John Gowers.* 1910.
Vising, J., *Étude sur le dialecte anglo-normand du XIIe siècle.* 1882.
—— *Le Purgatoire de saint Patrice des mss. Harl. 273 et Fonds fr. 2198.* 1916.

Studies of Proper Names :—
Barber, H., *British Family Names.* 2nd ed. 1903.
Gentry, T. G., *Family Names from the Irish, Anglo-Saxon, Anglo-Norman, and Scotch.* 1892.
Zachrisson, R. E., *A Contribution to the Study of Anglo-Norman Influence on English Place Names.* 1909 (with bibliography).
—— *Marylebone, Tyburn, Holborn,* in *M.L.R.,* xii. 146.

PART II

Gröber, *Französische Litteratur,* in *Grundriss der romanischen Philologie,* ii. 1902.
Gross, C., *The Sources and Literature of English History,* 2nd ed., 1915.
Gaston Paris, *La Littérature française au moyen âge.* 3rd ed., 1905.
Scargill-Bird, S. R., *A Guide to the various Classes of Documents in the Publ. Rec. Off.,* 1908.
Schofield, W. H., *English Literature from the Norman Conquest to Chaucer.* 1906.
Suchier and Birch-Hirschfeld, *Geschichte der französischen Literatur.* 2nd ed., 1913, vol. i.
Vising, *Sur la versification anglo-normande.* 1884.

Voretzsch, *Einführung in das Studium der altfranzösischen Literatur.* 2nd ed., 1913.
The Cambridge History of English Literature, vol. i. 1907.
Catalogues of Manuscripts.

ABBREVIATIONS OF TITLES

Arch. n. Spr. = *Archiv für das Studium der neueren Sprachen.*
Ausg. u. Abh. = *Ausgaben und Abhandlungen aus dem Gebiete der romanischen Philologie.* 1882 seq.
Berger, *La Bible* = Berger, *La Bible française au moyen âge.* 1884.
Bonnard, *La Bible* = Bonnard, *Les Traductions de la Bible en vers français au moyen âge.* 1884.
Bull. Soc. a. t. = *Bulletin de la Société des anciens textes français.* 1875 seq.
Deutschbein, *Stud.* = Deutschbein, *Studien zur Sagengeschichte Englands.* i. Teil. Die Wikingersagen. 1906.
Hist. Litt. = *Histoire littéraire de la France.*
Inc. = *Les Incipit des Poèmes français antérieurs au XVIe siècle,* par A. Långfors. 1917.
Jahrb. f. r. e. L. = *Jahrbuch für romanische und englische Literatur.*
Jahresb. rom. Ph. = *Kritischer Jahresbericht über die Fortschritte der romanischen Philologie,* i–xiii. 1890–1914.
Michel, *Rapports* = *Rapports à M. le Ministre de l'Instruction Publique sur les anciens Monuments de l'Histoire et de la Littérature de la France . . . par M. Francisque Michel.* MDCCCXXXVIII.
M.L.R. = *The Modern Language Review.*
Mod. Phil. = *Modern Philology.*
Not. et Extr. = *Notices et Extraits des manuscrits de la Bibliothèque Nationale et autres bibliothèques.*
Rel. Ant. = T. Wright and J. O. Halliwell, *Reliquiæ Antiquæ,* 2 vols., 1841–3.
Ro. or *Rom.* = *Romania.* 1872 seq.
Soc. a. t. = Société des anciens textes français.
Vising, *Étude* = Vising, *Étude sur le dialecte anglo-normand du XIIe siècle.* 1882.
Ward, *Catal.* = Ward, *Catalogue of Romances in the Department of Manuscripts in the British Museum,* i–iii. Vol. iii is by J. A. Herbert.
Z. f. fr. S. u. L. = *Zeitschrift für französische Sprache und Literatur.* 1879 seq.
Z. f. rom. Ph. = *Zeitschrift für romanische Philologie.* 1877 seq.

INDEX

OF ANGLO-NORMAN AND MIDDLE-ENGLISH AUTHORS AND WORKS

(The numbers refer to pages.)

Index of Authors and Works